Anti-Capitalism
A Beginner's Guide

ONEWORLD BEGINNER'S GUIDES combine an original, inventive, and engaging approach with expert analysis on subjects ranging from art and history to religion and politics, and everything in between. Innovative and affordable, books in the series are perfect for anyone curious about the way the world works and the big ideas of our time.

Anti-Capitalism
A Beginner's Guide

Simon Tormey

ONEWORLD

A Oneworld Book

First published by Oneworld Publications, 2004
Revised edition, 2013

Copyright © Simon Tormey 2013

The moral right of Simon Tormey to be identified as the Author
of this work has been asserted by him in accordance with
the Copyright, Designs and Patents Act 1988

ISBN 978-1-78074-250-2
Ebook ISBN 978-1-78074-251-9

Typeset by Cenveo
Printed and bound in Great Britain by
TJ International, Padstow, Cornwall, UK

Oneworld Publications
10 Bloomsbury Street
London WC1B 3SR
England

Contents

Acknowledgements

I need, firstly, to thank the team at Oneworld for their help and guidance since the inception of this project. It has been a source of surprise, delight and fear to find publishers who took such a close interest in what I was writing. Secondly, I'd like to thank the many individuals who chipped in with ideas, read portions of what I was writing or otherwise made my life easier. I should mention in particular Pete Waterman and Graeme Chesters, both of whom came out of the blue with interesting suggestions, papers and bibliographies. Easily my largest debt in this regard is, however, owed to Andy Robinson. As well as supplying a near constant stream of activist materials over the past few years, he has been a valuable 'sounding-board' for more or less every idea or theme that has found its way into the book. He also read and commented – in his own inimitable fashion – on crucial parts of the manuscript. Finally, I'd like to thank Véronique and our children, Max, Gabrielle and Louis for putting up with me and my numerous 'absences' when I should have been reading them a book or playing in the field. This book is dedicated to the original anarcho-situationist-beatnik, my mother, Patricia Tormey, who passed away just before work began on this revised edition. Some are given to write and think about life 'after' capitalism, and some people's lives embody what that might mean in practice. Patricia was one of those people. She is much missed by her friends and family.

Introduction

Anti-capitalism is not a new phenomenon. Indeed it is as old as capitalism itself, which most experts in the field would date from the rise of European mercantile or trading societies in the seventeenth and eighteenth centuries. On the other hand, popular interest in anti-capitalism, the kind of interest that drives commentators to write books about the topic, is new. It is new because until recently there was nothing that looked like an anti-capitalist movement, something that united all the disparate factions, groupings, ideologies and followers of 'the left'. Anti-capitalism, so it was held, was something that had died with the failed revolts of 1968, or with the Fall of the Berlin Wall or the 'Death of Communism'. Yet, piece by piece, event by event, these conclusions have been shown to be premature.

A number of key events over the course of the past couple of decades have encouraged many to conclude that there is, or might be, a global anti-capitalist movement. They include the Zapatista insurrection of 1994 that inspired numerous meetings and campaigns in solidarity; the Seattle protests of 1999; the creation of the World Social Forum in 2001; the wave of protests by the *Indignados* and the creation of the worldwide Occupy movement in 2011. Quite apart from these discrete yet always interconnected events and initiatives, there is a more general sense that anti-capitalism is 'in the air'. The Global Financial Crisis (GFC) of 2007 onwards punctured the impression of self-confidence amongst elites. It created uncertainty amongst commentators and experts about the 'inevitability' of capitalism, and thus created a chink of possibility for querying the desirability and necessity of capitalism itself. Figures such as Slavoj Žižek, a self-proclaimed Marxist and communist, were treated quite seriously by mainstream as well as alternative media. All manner of ideas and alternatives were given air time in a manner that was quite impossible to imagine before 2007. Indeed this author was invited to give a presentation at the 2010 OECD annual assembly on 'life after capitalism', something that would have been improbable a decade earlier, to say the least. Anti-capitalism has become part of the contemporary political climate. But what is anti-capitalism? What does it mean to be anti-capitalist? And where is anti-capitalism going – if anywhere?

As someone who has been teaching a variety of anti-capitalist subjects for two decades I have attempted to keep up with most things anti-capitalist over the course of that time. This was a fairly straightforward task until recently. Before then, 'anti-capitalism' meant looking mostly at the ideas and events of the past, sometimes the far-flung past. It also meant keeping abreast of the various activisms and ways in which apparently unfashionable ideas like socialism, anarchism and Marxism were supposed to be evolving, changing or adapting to New Times. 'Anti-capitalism' was a minority subject, in this case a very minor one compared with the more mainstream interests of some of my colleagues. The Seattle protests of 1999 changed all that. What we have witnessed since then is an enormous outpouring of analyses, commentaries and manifestos to go alongside the huge increase in activist materials, websites, newspapers and periodicals. Looking at the mountain of material out there, what is noticeable is that the work of those committed to saying something or writing about anti-capitalism tends to be of three kinds, some of which may be helpful *to* beginners, but few of which are *for* beginners. It will be useful to say something about what has been written so far, if only to give the reader a sense of what is already available, and also a sense of how I see my own task in relation to the existing literature on the subject.

Firstly, there are *activist orientated* books. These are books that are either written by activists *about* activism or written by activists *for* other activists (or would-be activists). These include the useful *Anti-Capitalism: A Guide to the Movement*. This is a cheap, well-produced account of the issues and events surrounding the re-emergence of anti-capitalism. It is published under the aegis of the British Socialist Workers Party (SWP), and many – though not all – of those writing commentaries or chapters are members of the Party. Those who are not are all activists of one kind or another and are able to give a good sense of the movement, where it has come from and where it is going. It is a good place to go for facts as well as a politically committed survey of developments. There are also reams of activist materials in activist outlets, some of which I list in the Resources section. If one really wants to get the 'worm's eye view' of what the anti-capitalist movement means to those who are part of it, then it would be indispensable to consult materials such as these.

Secondly, there are what might be termed *expert analyses*. These are works by people who have conducted research on some aspect or another of the contemporary global situation, together with a critique of it. The various writings of Naomi Klein would be one obvious place to start. Her book *No Logo* was a pathbreaking contribution of its kind, and rightly hailed as one of the key works helping to unpack the issues behind the corporate domination of the global marketplace. There are other works by investigative journalists-cum-activists that are also expert in this sense. Many will be familiar with the works of Michael Moore who, like Klein, has done much to highlight inequalities in his own country and the obstacles to the emergence of a progressive politics. Gregory Palast's *The Best Democracy Money Can Buy* follows Moore in offering a stinging exposé of contemporary politics.

Outside the US, the work of BBC journalist Paul Mason is well worth mentioning here, particularly as regards the impact of the GFC on the growth of political activism after 2007. His work on the origins and causes of the GFC is exemplary (*Meltdown:*

The End of the Age of Greed). He is also interested in the political effects of the GFC and the growth of anti-capitalism across the world in the wake of this latest crisis. His *Live Working or Die Fighting: How the Working Class Went Global* and *Why It's Kicking Off Everywhere: the New Global Revolutions* are indispensable for understanding the interplay of economic and political factors in the new radicalism. Still the most detailed account of the anti-capitalist movement itself – particularly the US movement – is Amory Starr's *Naming the Corporate Enemy: Anti-Corporate Movements Confront Globalization*, a comprehensive digest of all things 'anti-corporate' together with a critical evaluation of the various strengths and weaknesses of the movement.

In view of recent developments it is unsurprising to find that there is now a burgeoning literature of *post-capitalist advocacy*. These include outright 'manifestos' whose aim is to marshal the movement behind a particular political project or vision of how the world should look. Notable amongst these are Alex Callinicos's *An Anti-Capitalist Manifesto* and George Monbiot's *The Age of Consent*. The recent crisis of capitalism has also highlighted the availability of sophisticated theoretical treatments of the crisis and the availability of post-capitalist alternatives. Amongst these works, the most discussed would include the various contributions by Michael Hardt and Antonio Negri, starting with *Empire*, moving through *Multitude* and culminating with *Commonwealth*. One should also mention John Holloway's work *Change the World Without Taking Power*, and the follow-up work that takes account of the GFC, *Crack Capitalism*. Perhaps the most discussed theorist in this vein is Slavoj Žižek, whose work combines astonishing erudition, throwaway anecdotes from the communist era and reflections on film, popular culture and contemporary life. A prolific author of a number of works of importance for our topic including *Living in the End of Times* and *In Defence of Lost Causes*, Žižek is a very singular anti-capitalist figure, using the media, public events and activist causes to advance his reading of the present crisis. I discuss Žižek's work and the work of some of the other figures mentioned here in chapter 4.

So there is plenty to read out there. Why then do we need another book? As someone who spends a lot of time thinking, teaching and writing about anti-capitalism in one form or another, what is apparent is that there is nothing (yet) I could put in the hand of a student, friend, relative or neighbour and say 'here, this is quite a lot of what you might need to know about contemporary anti-capitalism. Here is an overview of the issues involved, together with a digest of some of the key arguments and issues'. This is to say there is nothing much for the *beginner* either in the sense of someone who wants to understand what is going on, or in the sense of someone who wants to begin acting but doesn't know *where* to begin. Here a word or two is needed about the notion of beginner underpinning the book.

I have thought hard about 'the beginner' to try to ensure that I keep within the remit of what my publishers want, but also because in a subject like this the notion of a beginner is ambiguous, handily so in the case of a topic like anti-capitalism. 'Beginners' can be passive or they can be active. They can, that is, be seeking to find out more about the anti-capitalist movement, why it came about, who is in it, where it is all heading. On the other hand they might be thinking 'something must be done', and be asking themselves where to find out more about the various resistances and campaigns going on. This is (hopefully) a book for both kinds of beginner.

I should say one more thing about the beginner and how it informs the kind of book I wanted to write. In my experience as a teacher beginners to a subject do not want to be told what the answers are, so much as what the *issues* are. They want a guide to a controversy, the ideology, the movement, the territory so that they can find their own way around in it. The worst teaching experiences I have endured (and indeed been responsible for) are those where an expert wears her politics on her sleeve. I don't like being harangued about a subject, or being told what to think or how to respond, and nor do most of those I have tried to help learn about a subject. This is not to say that I am neutral on the subject of anti-capitalism, as if one could be indifferent to the issues we will be discussing. I am not — and it will not take long for the reader to work out where I am coming from. Nonetheless, for the purpose of this book I have at least aimed at providing a *map* of the issues that will be of relevance to the interested beginner, not a set of *directions* pointing her to the 'right' place. This is not an activist work for activists; nor is it a manifesto or guide on how to change the world. It is a work by a specialist, but it is not an 'expert' analysis in the sense used above. I am not presenting new research or fieldwork designed to expose global inequities. What I have aimed for is a guide to the issues, positions, alternatives.

1

The hows and whys of capitalism

A question of definition

In a book about anti-capitalism we are naturally enough going to hear all sorts of reasons why it is that we should be opposed to capitalism. Many of these arguments will differ in sometimes surprising and indeed conflicting ways; but one thing they will all have in common is that they know what they are against: 'Capitalism' – or, more likely, refinements of the same such as 'neoliberal capitalism', 'transnational capitalism', 'economic globalisation', 'corporate capitalism'. Whilst anti-capitalist litera-ture is replete with reasons why one should oppose capitalism, they are often less helpful on what capitalism is and how it differs from other forms of social organisation. They are often less than forthcoming, too, on why it is that capitalism is 'hegemonic', why it appears natural or normal to so many (as it does). Thus what the beginner to the subject might already have asked him or herself is how it is that anyone came to think that capitalism was worth defending in the first place. So, thinking in terms of how to initiate the beginner into the nature of anti-capitalism, it is as good a place as any to start with some brief thoughts on *capitalism* itself. In particular we need to think about how capitalism estab-lished itself as a dominant economic system, and one accepted as rational and desirable by many across both the developed and developing world.

First of all it will be helpful to think about the central term capitalism itself. What exactly is capitalism? There are two ways of answering this question. The first is to think of it in *abstract* terms, that is in terms of what it represents as a relationship between people. The second is to think in more *historical* terms, i.e. of how it is that capitalism came about, and how it developed into the system we see before us today. Why do we need two ways of thinking about the same object? The easy answer is that since the dawn of capitalism in the early modern period (roughly the seventeenth century onwards) capitalism has obviously changed a great deal. Indeed it has changed so much that it is remarkable to be talking about the same 'thing' at all, the world of the twenty-first century being radically different to that of even the nineteenth century, let alone the seventeenth. Yet economists and commentators still agree for the most part that there is a fundamental continuity between then and now. What then is the continuity? Fortunately there is little controversy over the matter. Capitalism is not in this sense a particularly contested term in itself. What *is* contested is whether it is just, rational or otherwise in the best interests of humanity. In *abstract* terms it is said that we have capitalism where we see the following:

- private ownership over the means of production: land, factories, businesses;
- paid employment or, to put it another way, 'wage labour';
- creation of goods – or the offering of services – for profit via a system of exchange, i.e. the market.

This is a pretty anodyne definition, which is to say that most of those who take some professional interest in the matter would regard it with a shrug of the shoulders. This is what is intended. We are looking for a base line here: something that can be agreed on, so that we can understand exactly what it is that pro-capitalists celebrate and anti-capitalists object to. Looking at the definition other questions will, however, arise. Beginners as well as cynics might think that capitalism looks in this view utterly basic to human experience. What other kinds of economic relations might there be?

There is some substance to the concern, the chief among these being the relationship between capitalism and the market, or 'commodity production'. Hasn't there always been a market, and thus capitalism? The market or commodity production is indeed much older than capitalism, and there are those who would insist that virtually every society known to us embraced *some* form of market exchange, whether that be the exchange of shark teeth, beetroot or gold pieces. This is actually a very important point in relation to questions raised in relation to anti-capitalism, and so the need for clarity here is acute. The point is that the market is not an invention *of* capitalism, nor does the market of itself lead *to* capitalism. Markets have existed alongside all manner of different economic regimes and different forms of ownership. The mere exchange of equivalents does not necessitate or make inevitable wage labour, which is in turn the key to understanding the distinctiveness of capitalist production. Nor is the market in this sense something new or confined to capitalist economies. Markets have existed for longer than human history itself, which is not to say that the market is inevitable or necessary to human life as such, only that markets frequently arise in the course of human interrelationships, and will probably go on doing so as long as people want to swap things. But the point is, the market is not capitalism, and capitalism is not the market. So what is?

Looking back at the definition what becomes apparent is that one of the distinctive features of capitalism is that it serves a *particular kind* of market, namely that for labour. In pre-capitalist times labour was sometimes bought, but more often than not it was procured by some other means, classically by the institution of slavery, and more recently by bondage, vassalage, or other arrangement that rendered individuals directly subservient to someone else. Through force of arms, conquest, or some other more or less violent process people were made subjects of a lord or noble. As a slave or serf a person had little or no control over his or her own life, but rather was a mere adjunct of an 'estate' to which he or she was personally tied. As feudalism and slavery were overthrown or displaced, so those who were liberated became 'masterless' men (and women), freed to try and procure a living for themselves, usually through selling their labour to someone who needed it for the factories, mines and workhouses that accompanied the process of industrialisation. Here, in short, we see a process by which the economic relation of feudalism, namely control over the *person* is transformed into the capitalist economic relation in which some people buy other people's *labour power*. Whereas in the market place of Ancient Rome or of *ante bellum* America it was people who were bought and sold, in the capitalist market place it is our labour power that is bought and sold. But what is our labour power bought and sold for? Why do people need to buy and sell labour power?

Money, money, money

This brings us to the second relatively uncontroversial part of the definition of capitalism, which is that under capitalism the primary purpose of production is profit or making money. This too sounds a banal fact about the way we live. What on earth could be the point of setting up companies, working hard, taking risks, indeed getting up in the morning if it was not for making money?

We shall hear quite a lot more about what other ends production *could* serve when we come to discuss anti-capitalist ideas themselves, but for the purpose of contrast we could at this point think about one possible alternative to production as profit, which is production for what is termed 'subsistence'. It is probably a truism to note that over the course of human history most economic activity has been for the purpose of maintaining the well-being of the family and the extended groups of which the individual is a part rather than for making a profit as such. Looking closely at pre-capitalist production what is striking is the degree to which people worked just enough to ensure that they have the things they need to keep them going and to ensure that as and when unexpected crises come along (bad weather, poor crops etc.), there was enough surplus to ensure that everyone was looked after. This is what it means to subsist: a farmer works hard enough and long enough to make sure that all basic needs are met. Beyond that however, life is for living, singing songs, lazing in the sun, swimming, painting or whatever. Under such conditions profit has little rationale. To the subsistence farmer, profit requires extra work, and extra work means less time to do the other things she or he wants to do as well. This is one of the ironies of capitalist production spotted by the very earliest critics of capitalism. We often work harder and longer hours to be able to do the things that, if we worked less and for fewer hours, we would be able to do anyway, like lazing in the sun. So inevitably the question arises of why capitalism is characterised by production for profit as opposed to something else, like subsistence.

To answer this question we need to make a link between wage labour and profit creation, for what has yet to be clarified is why anyone would want to work for someone else rather than work for themselves as, say, a subsistence farmer. Why do most of us work for someone else, and not for ourselves, or for our families, or relatives or friends and neighbours, or with whom we choose?

Historically, the reason why most of us work for others is that we have very little choice but to do so. It is again a truism to note that in most parts of the world, *the* most important resource allowing a degree of independence to individuals, namely land, was conquered, invaded or otherwise taken from indigenous groups to serve the needs of royal families, *conquistadores*, colonial barons, imperial elites or states. In the UK the story of the creation of masterless men – or future 'employees' – is one that concerns conquest of a particularly crude, and at times bloody, kind over the course of the previous three centuries, and this is to say nothing of 1066 and the Norman conquest of Britain. Formerly independent subsistence farmers were thrown off the land, in turn forcing them into the towns and cities to search for work. We can note that some of the very first anti-capitalist protests and demonstrations were sparked off by such processes. They account in part for the sporadic resistances, sometimes violent, that punctuate modern British history, notwithstanding the impression given by conservative historians that Britain's historical development is a largely peaceful affair.

This is part of the story of the industrial revolution in Britain, and it is in turn part of the story of virtually every country the world over. It is part of the story of anti-capitalism in those countries that have experienced the failures of land reform in recent times. We could mention here the case of Mexico where the Zapatista rebellion of 1994 was initiated by those seeking a return of control over scarce arable land in the mountainous Chiapas region. We could also mention the Sem Terra, or landless, of Brazil striving for the means of getting land for those who have been deprived of it, or the Via Campesina network that attempts to help various groups restore their rights to land and agricultural produce. Much of Hugo Chavez's support in Venezuela came from the landless poor. But the story of the conquest of 'subsistence' is not the *whole* story, as those who defend capitalism will, with varying degrees of skill and urgency, insist.

We should also note, however, that the *private* ownership of the means of production is hardly intrinsic to human experience. For much of history, hunter-gathering was the norm and where this was displaced it was often by various forms of *collective* ownership, whether by families or kinship groups, or by larger units such as villages, towns and city-states. We can also note that even under advanced industrial conditions private ownership of production existed side-by-side with public ownership, as for example in the welfare or social democratic states of the early to mid-twentieth century. As recently as the mid-1980s over 50% of French GDP was accounted for by publicly owned enterprises. Even this ratio is dwarfed by the situation that obtained in communist states such as the former Soviet Union where the vast bulk of the productive capacity of the country rested in 'collective' hands, admittedly a euphemism for the party-state apparatus that ruled the country until its collapse in 1991. The private ownership of the means of production has thus historically *supplanted* a variety of other kinds of ownership, collective, communal and feudal. It also supplanted varieties of non-ownership, as in hunter-gathering and nomadic forms of life that subsisted without resort to ownership over the land and natural resources. It has also *co-existed* alongside rival forms of ownership, particularly the large-scale state ownership seen in the former communist bloc. Many if not all of these alternatives have some supporters amongst anti-capitalist groups, and so we will be returning to the issue of which, if any, of them, could provide a realistic and/or desirable alternative to the forms of ownership so many anti-capitalists object to.

So to summarise this brief discussion, we can talk about capitalism in abstraction from the historical conditions that brought it into being, but only just. Without some element of that history, we get the how, but we don't get the why, which is equally part of the case before us. We can see that capitalism is not the *same* as the market. Capitalism *is* of course a market society, but market societies may take forms other than those found under capitalist conditions. Even feudal and slave-owning societies were market societies. We can also see that capitalism requires a certain kind of social relation, namely that between formally free individuals. This means that wage labour is only possible where people are free to the extent of being able to sell their own labour power to someone else. People whose labour is forcefully taken from them are formally unfree like slaves or serfs. We can also see that capitalism is about the creation of profit. Profit is needed not least to give owners the money they need to keep themselves alive. It is also needed to reinvest in their businesses, in particular in the new technology and equipment that will enable them to compete successfully with others and thereby maintain those profits without which any capitalist enterprise will fail.

Capitalism as a system of competition

Though we have not mentioned it so far, this final point illustrates an important aspect of capitalism, which is that it is normally, though not necessarily, characterised by *intense competition*. Capitalism is as we know defined by the existence of a market; without a market there is no capitalism. A market is a physical or nominal space in which those with something to sell or exchange – like their own labour – can seek buyers. Much of the time there are others who will be wanting to sell something similar, and so there is a competition for buyers. What determines who wins the competition is, when all other things are equal, price. If I can sell tomatoes for a lower price than you can, I will sell more tomatoes than you.

The lower the basic costs, the lower, potentially, one can set the price of goods. So the tendency in market-based societies is competition on costs, *all* of the costs not just that of the labour power without which ultimately there can be no tomato farming. The seller who can reduce her costs, can reduce her prices further than the seller who has higher costs. This in turn means that in an environment of *intense competition* and relatively open markets that seller will be at an advantage: she will win the competition, driving her competitors out of business, into retirement or another sector of the market. That is until another tomato grower comes along who thinks she can reduce her costs *even further* (and so on).

What still needs clarification, however, is the difference between capitalist and non-capitalist forms of market competition. The tomato seller example used above illustrates some of what happens in markets as such, not just *capitalist* markets. Isn't there a difference? Indeed there is. As we have had occasion to note, a key to understanding capitalism is wage labour, and thus the competition for labour between capitalists. They need us, and in the absence of other means of keeping ourselves alive like having our own land, we need them. So the cost issue that we were discussing above refers very particularly to the costs of labour power and of keeping us working. This is much less the case in pre-capitalist societies where a great deal of production is based either on enforced labour of the feudal kind or on subsistence farming and manufacture which is characterised by family or small group production, rather than on wage labour. We have also noted that production in the capitalist market is for profit, with at least some of that profit being used for increasing the level of *productivity* through investing in machinery, new technologies, plant and equipment. So capitalism is a particularly *energetic*, or perhaps a frenetic, form of market society. Whereas the pre-capitalist market mainly concerns the reproduction of the basic necessities of life (give or take a few luxury goods) the capitalist market concerns the *accumulation* of capital though the exploitation of all available means for the increasing of production, whilst at the same time diminishing costs. Under the capitalist market there is no resting place for producer *or* seller. Capitalism is in its own self-image a Darwinian struggle, a struggle with many winners and many losers. It is for this reason that even Marx paused – part in admiration, part in incredulity – at the sheer relentlessness of the system, even whilst exclaiming how much he detested it.

Capitalism today

So far we have been describing capitalism in fairly *abstract* terms. That is, we have been trying to extract what it is that unites the very early forms of capitalist society with what we see around us today, but what we see around us Now is very different in many ways to what existed Then. It is time to think about what these differences are so we get a better sense of what capitalism is. This means thinking further about:

- interdependence and the transnationalisation of capitalism;
- corporate consolidation;
- the legal and political framework of economic globalisation;
- financialisation.

Towards a global (economic) village: interdependence and the transnationalisation of capitalism

It is no doubt true to say that capitalism has since its beginnings always been a world or 'global' system, in the sense that the rise of capitalism coincides with, and feeds upon, the rise of colonialism and inter-continental conquest. The markets of Europe in the sixteenth and seventeenth centuries were never in this sense merely markets for local produce, with local buyers and local sellers, but were supplemented with produce from colonies such as tobacco, wood and precious metals. But what is equally obvious is the degree to which, over the course of the development of the modern world, we see an ever-increasing *interdependence* between markets, producers and sellers. But what does this interdependence mean? What does it mean to be increasingly interdependent apart from the fact that there is more stuff to buy in the shops?

Thinking in terms of capital itself it becomes obvious that, over the course of the twentieth century, owners have removed capital, that is money, assets and resources from local, regional and national contexts in the pursuit of greater profit. Capitalists were once local people investing in local businesses, using local employment. This is no longer the case. Since the Second World War capital has become increasingly mobile, meaning that capitalists have been able to invest wherever they see the greatest possible return on their investment. They have been able to take advantage of ever-diminishing costs in terms of air freight, communications infrastructure and IT capabilities to outsource production to far-flung parts of the world. Such changes are often referred to in the specialist literature in terms of the transition from '*national* capitalism', to '*multinational* capitalism' and finally to '*transnational*' or 'global' capitalism proper. These labels give some idea of what is said to have occurred. The term 'globalisation' is more commonly used than any of these more specialist terms, but globalisation or, better, *economic globalisation* is just another way of talking about the same phenomenon, i.e. the growing interdependence of the world economy. Again, there is nothing new about global interdependence, as a glance at, say, Marx's *The Communist Manifesto* or Smith's *The Wealth of Nations* reveals. It is the *degree* to which we are interdependent that is striking and particularly so over the course of the last thirty years. But what does it all amount to?

We noted above that what determines the success or failure of the producer is her capacity to drive costs down to survive the intense competition that characterises the capitalist market place. Capitalists *must* do whatever they can to stay ahead of the game, which means being able to compete with others in the market place on price and cost. As we know costs vary from place to place and from country to country. In the global North the cost of living is pretty high. Housing costs are expensive. Thus the *basic* costs involved in producing anything are themselves relatively high, not least because of the high cost of keeping a worker working. By contrast, costs in the developing world are much lower.

Given *intense competition* it is irrational for capitalists not to take advantage of those conditions which aid the reduction of their costs. Why? Because if I can lower costs then *not* to do so will be to leave myself open to the possibility that someone else *will*, in turn putting me out of business. As a consequence, over the course of the latter third of the twentieth century capitalists engaged in a wholesale transfer of production from relatively expensive economies at what is sometimes termed the 'core' to relatively cheap economies at the 'periphery'.

So over the latter decades of the twentieth century capitalism became progressively *internationalised*, meaning that more and more production circled around the globe looking for the cheapest places to set up. Volkswagen went to Czechoslovakia, Spain, Poland; Ralph Lauren to Indonesia; Raleigh bikes to Thailand and Vietnam, and the really big corporations like Coca-Cola, Nike, Apple, Ford, Shell, McDonald's and Citibank just went anywhere and everywhere they could. This is what 'transnational' as opposed to 'multi-national' means. Multi-national corporations can be found in a number of countries; transnational corporations are by contrast ubiquitous. The concept of bounded locale as in 'national' is meaningless for them. They are *all over the world*. Thus the constraint of operating under local, regional, or national contexts in order to drive down costs has given way dramatically under the need to compete more effectively, which in turn leads to greater profit, and in turn to greater investment. All this is because it is (remember) in capital's *own* interest to seek the cheapest possible cost base, the cheapest resources and labour that it can find to produce the goods it wishes to produce. Such developments conform to what is sometimes termed the 'logic of capitalist accumulation'. To keep her business going the capitalist entrepreneur has to compete effectively, and this in turn means finding the most productive, most competitive, most commodious environment in which to operate. Not to do so is, as the history of contemporary capitalism painfully illustrates, to consign one's business to the dustbin of history. It was for this reason that even Marx argued there is little point in blaming *individual* capitalists for the character of capitalism. They are busy 'outsourcing', 'streamlining', down-shifting', 'flexibilising' because under a competitive market order they need to do whatever it is permitted to do to compete effectively. It is march or die.

Corporate consolidation: the big just got bigger

We noted earlier that in order to succeed in the market place you can either reduce your costs further than your competitors or you reduce the number of competitors through merger, incorporation or take overs. *Corporate consolidation* is a key part of the story of contemporary capitalism and helps explain why it has the character it has, and indeed why it is that the energies of so many anti-capitalists have been directed at the power of corporations. The degree of consolidations is indeed striking, particularly as regards older, capital intensive industries such as car manufacturing, shipbuilding or steel making. To take cars as an example, in the immediate post-war period there were literally dozens of manufacturers in Europe. Now one can count them on the fingers of two hands. But it is not just these traditional industries that have experienced accelerating consolidation. Look around the world of the media, luxury goods, software, drinks companies, banking. Everywhere one looks the story is the same: merger, acquisition, strip down, streamlining.

The survival of a multitude of brands in our shops does not, confusingly, obviate the point. Between them Unilever and Proctor and Gamble own hundreds of brands of soap powder, detergents and dishwasher tablets. The fact that the shelves of our supermarkets groan under the weight of an astonishing range of products should not be taken as a sign that there is an astonishing array of competitors out there in the market place for household

products such as these. There *was* an astonishing range of
competitors, but they became gobbled up by the 'big two' as part
of their efforts to shape the market place in accordance with their
own interests. Again, it seems we will be wasting valuable energy
blaming individual companies for looking after their own
interests in ways which are legal and part of the game. If there is
a fault to be found in this scenario then it lies with the rules of
the game, or rather with those who invent and maintain 'the
rules of the game'.

Here, however, matters get more complicated because the gap
between the 'players' and the 'makers of the rules' has narrowed
markedly to the point where we begin to see that often the
'players' and the 'makers' are the same people, albeit with different
'hats' on. In the case of large corporations such as Unilever, they
not only make soap powders, they also 'help' make the rules by
which international commerce is regulated (or not). As Michael
Moore, George Monbiot and Gregory Palast (amongst the many)
have documented, large corporations 'help' by buying the favour
of the political elites. They fund election campaigns, commercials
for local politicians, holidays for politicians, school fees, medical
fees, and lots of other useful services besides. They like things as
they are, and they are prepared to do a *lot* and spend a *lot* to make
sure that they remain so. This too is part of the game of contemporary capitalism.

The legal and political framework

Reflecting this latter point, one of the characteristics of contemporary capitalism is that it takes place within a *legal and political
framework* that is now, reflecting the internationalisation of trade
itself, global in scope. Here we need to mention those various
agencies and institutions set up by the most powerful states after
the War to oversee the development of international trade. Their
aim was to prevent the kind of economic instability seen in the

inter-war period, one that fatally undermined democracy in Germany and led to a severe crisis of confidence in the capitalist world more generally. The names of the institutions will be familiar to most people reading this book, as their various meetings tend to provide the pretext for anti-capitalist carnivals and protests, as for example at Seattle, Prague, Quebec City and Genoa. These institutions include the *International Monetary Fund* (IMF), The *G8*, the *World Bank*, and the *Organisation of Economic Co-operation and Development* (OECD). We need to mention too the various agencies of the United Nations involved in economic or socio-economic regulation, particularly the *United Nations Conference on Trade and Development* (UNCTAD). The *World Trade Organisation* (WTO) was set up much later in 1995 to provide a permanent institutional focus for the *General Agreement on Tariffs and Trade* (GATT) discussions which attempt to make the free market even 'freer', that is free from the barriers that prevent businesses circling around in perfect liberty.

What should be made clear is that it was the major capitalist states that set up these institutions, and they did so quite self-consciously to further their own *particular* interests (usually meaning nationally based economic interests), as well as the interests of capitalists *generally*, which is to say the interests of transnational companies like Unilever and Coca-Cola – no surprise there. Indeed it is hardly controversial to note that the rationale of these institutions is to make the life of capitalists as easy and uncomplicated as possible by facilitating the ability of capital to move freely, to compete on a 'level playing field', through currency reform, through opening up markets to competition and ensuring the flexibility of the labour market, which means reducing the cost to business of hiring and firing workers. This is all in the name of enhancing, promoting and facilitating the ability of capitalists to make profits, which is after all *why* they are in business. So it sounds like an easy ride for business. They, after all, designed and operate the institutions. But is it?

We'll learn more about this later, but just for the moment we need to return to what was just mentioned, namely the distinction to be drawn between the *particular* interests of capitalist states and the interests of capital *generally*. One of the fascinating aspects of the politics of international trade is that since the creation of these institutions it is evident that the gap between the particular and the general interests of capital has never been eliminated. This is to say that since the dawn of international trade there has always been a degree of friction between the demand for free trade and the desire of particular states to protect their own producers *from* free trade, usually through protectionist measures or tariffs, which are taxes that one country places on imports from another, usually in order to protect home producers from cheaper goods arriving from abroad.

One of the sources of greatest friction has been between those with relatively small-scale agricultural production such as France, and those with *either* large-scale agricultural production (such as the US) *or* with very cheap labour costs by comparison with the French *agriculteur* (such as the developing world). In practice this means that French (and EU) representatives lobby hard and long for protective tariffs for their agriculture, whilst at the same time bemoaning the fact that other people's markets are closed for the kind of goods that *they* produce at low cost relative to others. Meanwhile expensively subsidised cotton farmers in the US lobby hard to be allowed access to the markets of the developing world, whilst the US sets limits on the in-flow of steel, which it produces at high cost relative to countries such as South Korea. This leads to the practice of what is known as 'dumping', where producers in rich states who have received a government subsidy for manufacturing a commodity gain access to markets where the same commodity is produced at 'real' cost, i.e. without subsidy. The result is, for example, that sugar produced in the EU trades for less in many of the markets of the developing world than the latter's 'home' sugar. This in turn drives many producers in the developing world out of business, despite the fact that in 'real' terms they produce sugar much more cheaply than EU farmers. Such tragic outcomes are a direct correlate of the developing world's lack of bargaining muscle at the WTO where the detail of who can dump what on whom gets decided.

The position of the US and the EU is unsurprisingly crucial in the context of the development of international trade, yet it is a position that arouses controversy amongst globalisation watchers. The question that specialists in the field squabble over is this: when these two 'blocs' defend the interests of transnational corporations, do they do so from the position of wanting to defend their own *particular* interests, or from the point of view of the interests of transnational capitalist corporations, many of which are American or European in origin? Depending on one's answer to the question, globalisation will either appear like a neo-imperial project for the benefit of the wealthy North, or it will appear to be a process in which a global class (sometimes called the 'transnational capitalist class' or 'global economic elite') is in the process of detaching itself and its interests from national control, *including* the control of particular nation-states.

Squabbling between these various interests and dimensions of capital has been the pattern for better or worse since international trade became institutionalised. Where once protectionist measures were met with bombardments or a 'shot across the bows', now they are met with the huffing and puffing of expensively kept officials meeting in luxury conference centres. Nonetheless, this notion of the legal and political context within which capitalism operates is and will be an important one for our discussion, for what it implies is that, with *changes to the rules and regulations* of international trade, capitalism can be shaped according to different needs and interests. This is a source of hope for quite a number of anti-capitalists (particularly of the 'reform' variety), as it implies that the rules and regulations of international trade can be made fairer, and thus aid those who find their own interests or way of life at odds with those of big business. This is particularly so in the case of the very poor countries, which historically have done worst out of this post-war trade regime. Joseph Stiglitz, former Chief Economist at the World Bank, presents an alarming picture of just this kind of infra-warfare between representatives of global capitalism in his *Globalization and Its Discontents*, mostly (as he notes) at the cost of the development of the developing world.

Financialisation

In the first edition of this book written in 2003, I didn't mention the *financialisation of capitalism*. This looks not merely like oversight but negligence given that the Global Financial Crisis (or GFC) which started in 2007 was caused at least in part by the financialisation of the global economy. It was financialisation that led to profound economic shocks around the world, and a renewed bout of anti-capitalist protest and critique. So we need to make up ground quickly. What is financialisation and how does it connect to the themes of the book?

Financialisation describes the process by which banking and financial instruments come to have such a dominant influence on the rest of the economy that they determine the fate and fortune of all or most other sectors of the economy, such as production, agriculture, retail and services. This contrasts with the heyday of the industrial revolution where production was considered the motor of economic progress. It was shipbuilding, railways, cotton, agriculture and so on that made fortunes for businesspeople. Now it is hedge funds, credit default swaps and securitised instruments that dominate the news, that move the markets, that create crises and that determine whether an individual, a business and even a country will prosper, survive or decline. What happened to reverse the relationship?

This is a complex question. The easiest way to gain an insight into it is to look historically at the evolution of this trend towards a situation where the banks dispose of such huge sums of money that they were able to bring the capitalist system to its knees. What the story will tell us is that the increasing power of the banks and financial industry is strongly related to a decline in the scope and responsibility of *the state* in the wake of reforms designed to bring 'choice' and 'opportunity' to citizens – usually code for privatisations and the withdrawal of the state from the supply of what were formerly regarded as 'public goods'. Where once the state was, for example, responsible for looking after the savings and pensions of millions of citizens, that task now increasingly falls to banks and other financial bodies. States have privatised their funds, state banks, post offices. They have told citizens that their pensions are their own responsibility. They have encouraged local authorities to seek better returns with investment banks and more generally they have washed their hands of the responsibilities that go with the kind of 'cradle to grave' entitlements associated with the evolution of the welfare state. They have done this for a number of reasons, some ideological and some pragmatic.

Ideologically, the era of the 1980s and 1990s is synonymous with the rise of neoliberalism and the idea that 'personal choice' should trump the public interest. We were told that it was in our interest to look after our own savings and pensions rather than have the state do it for us. States have expensive bureaucracies, inflexible formulae for distributing goods, expensive fixed costs and rooms full of politicians who, when not lining their own pockets, like to raid our savings for their pet projects. So the newly empowered individual was meant to leave her savings with banks and building societies who would then invest her earnings to give a better return than anything manageable by the state.

Pragmatically, politicians felt it was too onerous to fund pensions out of taxation, particularly in countries with ageing populations such as in Europe and Japan. Better to divest the state of long-term responsibility for funding retirement than to ask a weary electorate for more taxes.

So the state 'retreated', or was forced to retreat by international agencies encouraging the 'restructuring' of fiscal policies. As a result more money found its way to the banks. In a context of *intensifying competition* the banks searched the globe for the best returns, which in turn gained them more clients and higher profits. All this was aided by the technological revolution that translated into increasingly automated purchasing in the key markets. Banks could shift billions of dollars from one currency to another with the click of a button. Moving billions around the currency and futures markets on the hypothesis that one currency is about to gain a tiny percentile increase against another results in handsome profits at the flick of a switch. Seeing this, investors became much more interested in buying into banks than into the manufacturing industry, where the returns take longer, and are much less spectacular.

Credit thus flowed through the markets in the 1990s and early 2000s. Banks had plenty of money to lend. The problem became one of finding the individuals and businesses that could use the credit and earn a return for the banks in the form of interest. The easier it becomes to find credit, the more banks have to compete on the basis of risk. If all the high-earning individuals already have the credit they need and want, banks have to turn to the less wealthy. As this process develops so banks end up lending to those with very little income – but of course in return for greater rewards. 'High net worth' individuals will pay the money back; 'sub-prime' individuals (and businesses, and countries) might not. Hence higher interest can be charged with the promise of greater returns for the banks. Or so the theory goes.

At this point the story gets more interesting because the explosion of credit only gives us a part of the story of financialisation. The other part of the story is the explosion of the instruments devised in order to maximise profits for banks and for the individuals who work for them. The terms are on one level technical and sober-sounding: 'credit default swaps', 'collateralised debt obligations' (CDOs), 'structured investment vehicles' and suchlike. The idea of 'derivative' products such as these is to make it easier for banks to buy and sell debt, to insure themselves against bad debt ('securitisation') and generally to take on additional risk with the promise of additional rewards. BBC financial journalist Paul Mason estimates that in 1998 the market for CDOs was around $1 trillion – a lot of money. By 2008 the market was worth $58 trillion. This was no longer banking; this was gambling with huge sums of money temporarily borrowed to 'leverage' massive future gains. How did this happen? Who let it happen?

Banks used to lend an individual money, say, to buy a house, and charge them interest on the loan, making themselves a profit that could then be used to lend to others – and of course pay for the banks' employees and costs. Over the course of the 1980s and 1990s banks increasingly bundled up packages of debt and sold it on to others. So instead of dealing with thousands of individuals, banks could buy millions of dollars' worth of debt that yielded a certain interest rate. The riskier the debt, the higher the return. So here the debtor/debtee chain which was once a two-way relationship (bank/individual) is extended to include third, then fourth parties and so on (bank/intermediary/individual; bank/intermediary/intermediary … /individual). Each link of the chain takes on higher risk for potentially greater rewards. The British bank Northern Rock once used to lend to thrifty folks in the north of England. They had steady, but not spectacular, returns for a century or so (or rather the two banks which merged to create Northern Rock in 1965 did). Then along came a clever banker called Adam Applegarth who promised to spice things up a little and generate much greater returns for the board by taking on debt from, amongst other sources, Latin American mortgages bundled up in derivatives. The results were spectacular – for a while. Northern Rock's results took off along with its exposure to risk. However, when the risks started to turn sour, as they did over the course of 2007, so matters began to spiral out of control, to the point where by 2008 it was clear that the UK had its first bank 'run' in 150 years.

What was true for Northern Rock was true for banks across the US and the UK. In the US the problem was more directly related to sub-prime mortgages at home than abroad. Over the course of the 1990s a property boom had convinced bankers of the wisdom of lending to individuals in low income, temporary or precarious employment, on pensions, or without an established credit history. Credit was extended to those who were unlikely ever to pay it back on the basis that the underlying asset, or property, would be gaining in value and thus that the risk of default would be offset by the asset, which could be sold on to cover losses. As the property bubble popped, so this risk equation collapsed, leaving some of the largest financial organisations in the US hopelessly exposed. Freddie Mac and Fanny Mae, amongst the largest mortgage lenders in the US, collapsed. AIG, the insurance giant that underwrote many of the mortgages, nearly went under. Companies such as these, worth hundreds of billions of dollars, were going bust overnight. This led to turmoil on the markets and a 'credit crunch', leaving banks without the means of accessing the credit they need in order to lend to clients. The global financial system found itself under such strain that only a major injection of liquidity or electronic money from outside the system would stave off collapse. Where was that liquidity to come from?

Ironically the source of salvation at this moment of extreme crisis of open markets and financialisation was the one entity that apologists for this 'financialised' form of capitalism had much earlier identified as an obstacle to freedom and economic growth: the state. It was the state that put in place cumbersome regulatory measures limiting the amounts banks could borrow. It was the state that insisted on regular audits, accountability of 'principals', measures to prevent and detect corruption and suchlike. Throughout the 1990s and 2000s politicians came under huge pressure to relax these regulations, to smooth the path of 'liquidity' in the name of allowing the banks to utilise every opportunity to maximise returns. Gordon Brown, Chancellor of the UK Exchequer, famously called this period 'the golden age of banking', indicating in direct terms his approval of the direction of travel. The same sentiments could be heard in the US where politicians of both sides were complicit in removing a regulatory framework that had taken decades of hard bargaining to put together to safeguard the public interest. Yet within months the golden age had crashed and burned. Surveying the wreckage of the GFC, politicians across the industrialised world were compelled to step in to avert a complete wipe-out of savings, mortgages, individual and national wealth, indeed money itself. One banker in the UK was so convinced that money was about to lose all value reported to the Chancellor that he had bought a flock of sheep to tide his family over with food whilst the crisis played out.

One point became obvious in the course of the crisis: whereas banks cannot print their own money, states can, through selling bonds or 'gilts' as in 'gilt edged' loans. States can do this because unlike banks they have the power to tax citizens and thus ensure that someone will ultimately pick up the tab. At a moment of severe systemic crisis, as witnessed in the GFC, the ability of states to print money (in the form of 'quantitative easing' or QE), ensured an easing of the credit crunch, a ready source of liquidity for banks and other financial intermediaries and thus a normalisation of inter-bank lending that permitted the world as we know it to carry on. But the world had changed, as had our understanding of the relationship between economics and politics.

Neoliberalism: beginning of the end or end of the beginning?

With the GFC neoliberalism had suffered its first major crisis. It had survived; but only just – and the vision of the world it promoted was damaged. Whether the damage is irreparable remains to be seen; but the effect of the crisis was to remind us that neoliberalism is far from the omnipotent project it has seemed to both supporters and critics since Reagan, Thatcher and their allies took office in the 1980s and 1990s. On the contrary, neoliberal certainties, such as the need for open markets, free flow of capital, deregulation of financial instruments, and the shift of risk from the state to the individual, were left in tatters by the GFC. Cracks had appeared in the edifice. An ideology had been discredited, even if the propagators of the ideology were still in power. How to cope with the existential crisis as well as the financial one? How to ensure that the basic structures of power and wealth were maintained intact even if the 'certainties' were not? In the wake of the GFC elites had to decide whether to retreat or drive on.

The contrast between the US and the UK is instructive in this respect. In the US Obama's QE programme served to revalue the role of the state in underpinning economic activity, as did the billions of dollars poured into ailing banks, car makers and other strategically important industries that might otherwise have gone to the wall. If not a return to social democracy, the actions of the Federal Reserve and the President served to provide a counterpoint to the decades of neoliberal commentary that insisted that the state was complicit in undermining industry and economic life more generally by providing subsidies and financial support for the 'unproductive'. Here the subsidies served to bail out the neoliberals sitting on the boards of the major banks, insurance companies, and corporations. Little wonder we heard less about the destructive impact of the state. In the UK, elites took the opposite tack. Using the politically convenient fact that it was the Labour Party that swamped the markets with cash enabling banks to keep going, the incoming coalition administration immediately embarked on a programme familiar to readers of Naomi Klein's *Shock Doctrine*, a powerful critique of neoliberal ideology and its application to the developing world. Here, however, the object of the experiment was not Russia or South-East Asia, but a G7 major economy.

As tends to happen at such moments, critical movements and ideas gained a currency that hitherto seemed unimaginable. The sporadic anti-capitalist events and initiatives of the 1990s and early 2000s, the Zapatista insurrection, the Seattle protests, the subsequent 'carnivals against capitalism' gave way to a more persistent mood of defiance, resistance and opposition on behalf not just of a fringe of activists or indigenous insurgents, but of ordinary men and women appalled by the spectacle of taxpayers' money being used to bail out wealthy bankers and financial institutions.

Politics, as a contest of ideas, as a field of contingency or open-ness, had returned. Or rather it had moved out of the underground into the spaces and places of the global wealthy. Resistance has moved from a subterranean activity hidden in the nooks and crannies of the world system, to the very epicentre of global capitalism. History had not 'ended'. Capitalism had not triumphed. Politics had not been transcended or rendered redundant. On the contrary, with the GFC, anti-capitalism was about to go mainstream.

2
Anti-capitalism after the 'end of history'

In a brilliantly polemical essay published in 1989 entitled 'The End of History?' Francis Fukuyama suggested that with the fall of the Berlin Wall history had in some important sense come to an 'end'. What he meant was not that history as 'the passing of time' had ceased or that important events would somehow be prevented from happening. What he wanted to suggest was rather that the philosopher Hegel's idea of history as having an end or goal was about to be vindicated in *political* terms. Fukuyama saw something that many others were to comment upon, which is that, with the fall of the last great ideological crusade, communism, there was now a more or less tacit consensus that liberal-democracy was the best or most desirable political system. Liberal-democracy had emerged victorious from the Cold War, indeed, from the more fundamental clash of ideologies that characterised the post-Enlightenment world. Ideological conflict was a thing of the past. We were all liberal-democrats now.

Then in the winter of 1999 came the 'battle of Seattle'. In one week – if not in one day – the appearance of consensus concerning the ends and goals of western civilisation disappeared in a great clamour of dissensus, of protest, of confrontation between the forces of liberal-democracy and the forces of an as yet unnamed some-Thing that was most certainly *not* liberal-democratic. Seattle was itself a mere prelude to the emergence of a new wave of protest that encompassed demonstrations at the G7/8 and WTO, the growing militancy of oppositional movements in the global South, the emergence of the World Social Forum, the *Indignados* and latterly Occupy. Part of the contemporary interest in anti-capitalism is understanding how a movement or tendency that seemed to have 'died' appeared to re-emerge so vigorously to confound expert commentators such as Fukuyama. Where, it needs to be asked, did Seattle and the new wave of militancy come from, and why did it take the various forms that it did?

SEATTLE: WHAT HAPPENED?

As we noted in the introduction, many commentators, both activist and non-activist, regard the Seattle protests of December 1999 as the moment when the contemporary anti-capitalist/anti-globalisation movement was born. Why? On the face of it, Seattle was just like many other protests in recent years. A meeting of the WTO provided the pretext for a mass demonstration – but such protests have been regular events since the Rio Earth Summit of 1992. What was different about Seattle was, firstly, the *diversity* of groups present, and also the presence of trade unions which had been signally absent from the major protests particularly in North America up to this point. 'Teamsters' or union activists met with 'Turtles' or environmental activists in a great activist melting pot. Secondly, there was the *nature* of the protest. The authorities in Seattle were determined not to be shown up as 'weak' in the face of a major protest involving up to 70,000 people, and thus deployed a heavy-handed approach to policing. This led to violent confrontations, involving the use of teargas and baton rounds, providing dramatic, heavily mediatised images that seemed to signal the radicalisation of activism. The *effect* of the policing was in fact to promote greater solidarity between different groups which might otherwise never have spoken to each other. Debates and discussions were staged, alliances forged, networks created. Perhaps most dramatically of all, the protests actually succeeded in shutting down the meeting of the WTO, thereby giving the impression that large scale mass action could achieve something more than a temporary discomfort to global elites. They could disrupt global capitalism in some very tangible manner. The Seattle protests thus promoted the notion that large demonstrations were an important and immediate way in which neoliberalism could be combated.

Trying to account for a phenomenon as complex and varied as anti-capitalism will inevitably involve a simplification of complex social forces and currents. Nonetheless the impatient beginner will want to know *something* of those forces and currents, even if we can only approximate the manner in which they interact and flow into each other. Here Fukuyama can be of service, because what he offers is an account of why it is that the emergence of a radical counter-consensual current had become *unthinkable*. By simple deduction we can infer that if the outcome of his prediction was wrong, then elements of the reasoning must have been wrong. Looking closely at the contention he offered, we can point to two key assumptions that Seattle and subsequent events were to problematise:

1. that liberal-democracy had the capacity to manage the effects of the processes outlined in the last chapter, particularly the transformation of capitalism from being essentially national in character, to being transnational or global;
2. that an oppositional *politics* necessarily stems from an oppositional *ideology*, and thus that with the 'death of communism' – if not the death of ideology as such – *oppositional* politics would wither.

With regard to (1), what becomes obvious with hindsight is, paradoxically, that the qualities celebrated in liberal-democracy by thinkers such as Fukuyama are those most under threat by these macro-economic developments. Indeed, it is little exaggeration to say that if anything triumphed in 1989 it was not 'liberal-democracy', but global capitalism. This is to say that it was not politics that triumphed over economics, as implied in Fukuyama's analysis. It was a case of *economics triumphing over the political*. Thus it might be argued that the anti-capitalist 'battle of Seattle' represented 'a return of the political', a return of ethics, morality and values in place of the vacuum created by the departure of politics from the global scene. This sounds more like a conclusion than a premise, so let's take two steps back and attempt to unpack these arguments. This will help us to get a sense of the broader significance of the emergence of an anti-capitalist movement post-Seattle and will in turn help us to see what potential lies within it for the recuperation of politics itself.

Problems of liberal-democracy

As a sometime teacher of Soviet politics, I used to refer to a journal entitled *Problems of Communism*. The agenda of the journal was contained in its title. Communism had of necessity 'problems' that it was the journal's task to analyse. There is no equivalent journal of liberal-democracy, which is not to say that liberal-democracy is problem-free, because the problems of liberal-democracy are not (yet) held by mainstream political scientists to be fundamental or intrinsic to its very operation, as were communism's 'problems'. Yet, as should be clear from the discussion of neoliberalism in the previous chapter, developments over the past thirty years necessitate a reappraisal of this position. Indeed it is hardly hyperbole to suggest that the presuppositions informing liberal-democratic theory are now threatened with redundancy and need to be rethought. Why is this?

Firstly, it is evident that we are in the midst of *a crisis of liberal-democratic politics*. The emergence of anti-capitalist currents and initiatives is a symptom of that crisis. In particular it is a sign that not enough is being done at the national level to convince concerned individuals that political actors are capable of influencing, let alone controlling, economic actors. This is not the same as saying that the *nation-state* itself is in crisis, which is implied in much of the commentary on globalisation. Unlike their territorial forbears, the empires of the late nineteenth century, nation-states are *not* in danger of disappearing, and of course as we saw in the previous chapter states played a crucial role in staving off the collapse of the global financial system during the GFC. If anything, the GFC revalorised the role of the state particularly as regards providing a stable source of funding for banks. Indeed, it was the very lack of a regulatory regime in countries most in thrall to neoliberal ideology that led to financial crisis in the first place. On the other hand it is also clear that nation-states are all too often taken hostage by forces, principally transnational corporations, that are able to apply considerable pressure to ensure that their every whim is catered for. This undermines and weakens the sense that politics has at the nation-state level. For politics to be effective and relevant it has to be able to shape or affect the behaviour of the economic actors who do so much to determine the character and prospects of modern societies. 'Justice' is what we as a political community say is just, and what we say is just must in turn be able to be translated into just policies. Problems begin when the community has little or no control over its own affairs, when it is unable to govern itself in accordance with its own wishes. Liberal-democratic thinkers like to describe liberal-democratic politics as, in essence, one of self-government. 'We' (or rather our representatives) 'govern', and the state as the executor of our decisions carries out whatever it is we want it to do. Liberal-democratic states are *described* as governing themselves ('government of the people, by the people, for the people'). The *reality* is rather different, as the people of Greece, Ireland and Portugal have found out in the wake of the sovereign debt crisis in Europe in 2011–12. What happened?

Recall the last chapter: one of the most important developments of the last third of the twentieth century is the transformation of capitalism from being largely national in character, to being multi-national and then transnational or *global* in character. Much of what we term capitalism, particularly the capitalism of the major corporations, is conducted beyond or outside the direct control or influence of the nation-state. Indeed the major corporations conduct themselves in a 'state-like' manner (if not a 'statesman-like' manner), acting upon their *own* self-interest as opposed to the interests of the nation associated with the company or brand. One difficulty in terms of the problematic being discussed here is very evidently that the process propelling us towards *economic* globalisation has not hitherto been matched by a process of *political* globalisation, leaving a marked 'democratic deficit' between the two spheres. This is in contrast with the way that the process of the construction of *national* capitalism was matched – and in cases like France, *preceded* – by the construction of a *national state* implying that the activities of economic actors could, at least in theory, be shaped or determined in accordance with political priorities as well as economic ones. Here we need to make two further observations.

Firstly, global capitalism is subject to a legal and political framework; but this framework does not of itself constitute a 'state' as that term would usually be understood, that is as a sovereign power with the capacity to act independently of the particular interests within. The institutions of global governance are at present subject to corporate needs and interests, rather than the other way round. Whether they might be so constituted as to act like a state is a matter of heated debate within anti-globalisation circles, for reasons that will become more apparent in the next chapter. Secondly, those political bodies that *do* claim quasi-sovereign character, such as the UN, are without the means of controlling the activities of global economic actors, let alone those states which choose to ignore the decisions of the

UN unless it suits them to do otherwise, which happens to include states such as the US. As the diplomatic run-up to Gulf War II showed, the UN is in any case only at best a quasi-sovereign body, and even this status has now to be considered as one dependent on the indulgence of the US. The net result is that whilst the domain of political authority has remained at the nation-state level, the domain of economic activity has increasingly shifted to the global level. There is *no global state* and there is no effective mechanism of *accountability* for those actors that operate at the global level, such as global corporations. The latter exist in a sort of postmodern state of nature directly accountable to no one but themselves and the shareholders of the company.

Such a situation implies that the economic domain has become ever more detached from political control and thus that the relevance of the state as a primary site for democratic decision-making is becoming diminished by the day. It is this observation that underpins the '*death of the nation-state*' thesis which has been vigorously debated by political scientists and commentators since the late 1980s, i.e. just at the moment when Fukuyama wrote so glowingly of the 'triumph' of liberal-democracy. Now, whether or not the nation-state really is 'dead' need not detain us for long (it isn't). What we need to note is that the debate is usually framed in terms of the *degree* to which the state can be said to be becoming irrelevant, not on the more general thesis that the state is 'losing power' vis-à-vis economic actors, and indeed vis-à-vis supra-national bodies such as the EU. For our purposes the more salient point is that the process by which capital became transnational created a political vacuum which is felt today in a number of ways that can help explain the re-emergence of anti-capitalist ideas and initiatives. These might be summarised as: the *decline of ideological difference* and the *decline in democratic participation*. It is 'official' politics that has borne the brunt of the vacuum created by the 'hollowing out' of the state.

The end of ideology (revisited)

Firstly, what is evident is that the *ideological differences* between political parties and thus between governing elites has diminished to the extent that many wonder what the point of party politics is. This is not to say that the ideological divisions between the parties were in the past more significant than their similarities, as is sometimes implied in the commentary. As has long been noted, the tendency of electoral politics is to reduce ideological difference in an attempt to capture the centre-ground where the average voter can be found. Thus it might be considered normal for ideological differences to be ironed out over the long term in response to the need to broaden the appeal of a party for electoral purposes. Nonetheless, it is important in terms of the *self-image* of liberal-democratic politics that voters perceive that there is a significant difference between parties, and thus that there be some element of choice as between different visions of how the country should be governed. Commentators have long remarked on the basic similarity in ideas between the Republican Party and the Democrat Party in the US; but those same commentators have often smugly noted the much deeper ideological cleavages apparent in European politics. As regards the US, the Republicans and Democrats have long traded on their different concerns and values, the former standing up for entrepreneurial dynamism, the centrality of family and community, and a muscular view of America's place in the world. The latter, by contrast, championed the poor, those from ethnic or racial minorities, those otherwise overlooked in the individualistic pursuit of the Dream. Yet such differences are now less significant than the similarities between the two – particularly when in power. Both parties are at their very core pro-corporate, pro-market, pro-individualism.

In the UK the Labour Party was seen as the champion of the working class and of social democratic or welfarist policies. Now the Labour Party, or, New Labour, is the party of privatisation, 'private finance initiatives' (PFIs) and the private funding of hospitals, schools and roads. In this sense the coming to power of New Labour in 1997 hardly represented a break with the Conservatives, the party that introduced a neoliberal agenda. Indeed, many of the more controversial policies brought in by the latter were not merely endorsed, but driven on by the new administration, as for example in the case of the privatisation of the railways, reform of the health service and the introduction of tuition fees in higher education. This in turn fuels the *perception* that there is little to choose between Labour and Conservative, and thus the growing redundancy of party politics itself.

What goes for Britain equally goes for many other advanced industrial countries such as France, Australia and Germany. Around the world ideological cleavage has given way to the neo-liberal orthodoxy described in the previous chapter, one built around the 'necessity' for low inflation, flexible labour markets, balanced budgets, privatisation and competition in all areas of public activity. This situation is a reflection of the dominance of corporate interests that demand such conditions in return for the internal investment that brings jobs, wealth, and 'opportunity'. This is presented as less the result of a contest between unequal parties, namely the nation-state and global corporations, and more as the result of the 'prudent' and 'realistic' assessment of national interests by our representatives.

Anyone for voting?

As ideological cleavages have diminished (or are perceived to have diminished) so we have seen, secondly, a *decline in political participation* at the official or national level. This means a decline in voting, party membership and a more general but equally dis-cernible decline in interest in national, supra-national *and* sub-national or local politics. Recent voting statistics in the UK as elsewhere make for gruesome reading for those concerned about the legitimacy of electoral politics, with turnouts heading below the 30% and even the 20% mark for local elections and elections to the European parliament. In the US the Presidential election attracts just half of all eligible voters. At Congressional level the weariness of the electorate is even more impressive, with turnouts on a par with those recorded for European elections in the UK – to say nothing about elections at state and county level, which barely register a flicker on the radar of the electorate.

In a similar vein, the memberships of all major parties in the UK are in free-fall, precipitating a financial crisis, in turn pushing them further towards corporate sponsorship. The Conservatives boasted over 2 million members in the 1960s. Now it has in the order of 300,000 members. Membership of the Labour Party halved between the triumphant landslide of the 1997 general election and its defeat at the 2010 election. Meanwhile political coverage in the media is being continuously remodelled to appeal to 'youth'; but it seems that 'youth' has got better things to do with itself than listen to the old and wise telling them how important it is to participate in official politics. Similar phenomena are well-documented across the western world and point to the decline in the perceived importance of the nation-state as the site of political contestation. Whoever we vote for, 'they' always win.

The net result is the *crisis of liberal-democracy* confronted with economic forces that are largely beyond the reach or control of national governments. For our purposes this translates into a crisis of 'official' politics, that is, the politics of political parties, of elections and participation in the mainstream political process, compelling those who really *are* concerned about the state of the world into more 'unofficial' or subterranean forms of engagement. Who are these people? As implied in the comments above, we need to think here in *horizontal* terms, that is in terms of *ideological affiliation* along the spectrum of political beliefs; and also in *vertical* terms, or in terms of the reach of politics from the global level down through the supra-national, then national and sub-national levels.

If the tendency of electoral politics is to push the main parties towards the centre, then this leaves behind a significant number of participants who are alienated by the spectacle of the land grab at the middle, and thus of the necessary watering down of political demands to seek the acceptability of the party in question. This is a phenomenon that affects both the left and right of the political spectrum. Indeed, one of the tendencies of contemporary politics is the seeking of alternative outlets for both radical leftists *and* radical rightists, sometimes with perverse results. There are also the missing voters who have either given up politics altogether or moved underground, choosing to dispense altogether with electoral politics in favour of campaigning and direct action. So the *perception* of ideological consensus around neoliberal policies has served to jolt people out of the regular political habits that liberal-democratic theorists regard as key to the legitimation of the political process. Increasingly, radicals have chosen to abandon the fight *within* official political parties for control over the ideological agenda and formed their own groups outside the political mainstream.

On the *vertical* plane, that is the plane between the global level of politics at one end and the local at the other, we see an analogous process taking place. This is to say that the perceived inability of political parties and other official actors to influence or shape politics at the global level encourages concerned individuals to seek unofficial means for pursuing their ends. Those particularly animated by the issue of global justice and the inequalities between the Global North and the Global South have found it increasingly futile to pursue these concerns through political parties whose rationale is, traditionally, to preserve and enhance the interests of a given *national* territory. On these terms it has become much more relevant (and much more rewarding) to join one of the proliferating unofficial or DIY ('do it yourself') groups whose mission is to remind the global wealthy of their obligations to the poor and indebted. In short, the vacuum we noted above with regard to the absence of global political bodies with the clout and presence to bring global economic actors to account could only be met through *unofficial* political action. How better to advance those claims than to turn up at the meetings of the WTO, the World Bank or the G8 and seek redress directly, immediately, *now*?

The same can be said for politics at the local or community level. Official local politics may be in crisis, but the vacuum created has permitted a range of independent voices to be heard in elections, as well as a range of community level initiatives to be unleashed. Such initiatives are not merely outside the mainstream; they challenge it in very direct terms. The evident vibrancy of women's groups, environmental activism, local protests at the closures of hospitals, schools and local services, road-building and housing projects all underline the degree to which the crisis of official politics marks the growing importance of a different kind of politics: a disaggregated, diverse plurality of disparate actions and initiatives. Politics *in this sense* is alive and well. It has simply moved off the official political stage. Such a politics will remain subterranean and invisible to elites and the metropolitan media. Until it erupts.

1968 and the crisis of oppositional politics

The above point underlines a further difficulty of Fukuyama's confident analysis. This is the assumption that a meaningful oppositional politics is one that has to be framed in terms of an official ideology of opposition, in this case communism or Soviet Marxism. Fukuyama's assumption, shared by the global elite, was that the defeat of communism would provide a basis for a new consensus on the desirability of liberal-democracy, and indeed of capitalism.

And it is easy to see why they might have been lulled into thinking in such reductive terms even when, as is now obvious, the defeat of communism was actually a key factor permitting the *emergence* of an anti-capitalist movement. If this sounds paradoxical then we need to note that the Cold War made for a very simplified politics. The world was divided by an elite-driven discourse into two camps: those who defended 'freedom', or capitalism (the two being the same in elite Cold War-speak), and those who did not. The latter were 'communists' who had to be confronted and defeated in order to protect freedom. This simplification of politics served an essential function for both the US and the Communist Bloc. It allowed the former to demonise oppositional politics as 'communist' and thus to tar oppositionists with the brush of being traitors to the cause of freedom more generally. On the other side of the fence it gave legitimacy to the communists' claim to be fighting on behalf of the world's poor and oppressed. It thus annexed oppositional activity to the interests of the Soviet Union in particular. There was nothing like a 'third space', a space in-between these blocs, creating countless dilemmas for progressives and political radicals until the collapse of the Soviet Union.

What this global picture hid was in fact more important than what it revealed. What had become evident much earlier than 1989 was that the Soviet Union's claim to represent the cause of anti-capitalism was essentially bogus. Considered in terms of the prospects of the development of an oppositional politics in the West, it is clear that the 'Soviet road' was widely, if not universally, recognised as a dead-end after 1968. Indeed it was, more gener-ally, the astonishing events of 1968 that showed the direction in which any anti-capitalist resistance was likely to go. Here we can touch upon three developments of significance for thinking about the contemporary anti-capitalist movement:

1. the final loss of credibility of the Soviet Union itself as the official agent of anti-capitalism;

2. the significance of the Paris *Évènements* as a challenge to the official Marxist-Leninist narrative of liberation; and

3. the displacement of an official oppositional politics by the proliferating *unofficial* politics of new social movements and special interest groups.

The Prague Spring and the end of Soviet Marxism

To begin with the *position of the Soviet Union*, 1968 was the year of the Prague Spring when the efforts of the reform-minded leadership of Czechoslovakia were brutally crushed by Soviet intervention. Alexander Dubcek had under pressure from 'people power' introduced a series of reforms dubbed 'socialism with a human face', which eased considerably the otherwise stifling rule of the Communist Party. Fearing that such measures – including greater freedom of speech and the granting of certain minority rights – would quickly lead to the demand for similar policies in the rest of the Communist Bloc, the Soviets ordered their allies in the region to join in an armed intervention to overturn Dubcek's regime. The hardliner Gustav Husak was installed and he rapidly overturned the liberal reforms. This was not of course the first such intervention to snuff out the challenge of reformism. The most hideous of them all occurred in Hungary in 1956 where Imre Nagy had attempted to introduce a liberalisation of the Stalinist measures of forebears such as Mátyas Rakosi. But the crushing of the Prague Spring had a very particular resonance for much of the Western Left. It was the final collapse of the now vain idea that the Soviet Union could be a force for good in the world; that somehow it represented the hope for a better world. The Soviet Union was finally revealed as just another form of brutal elite rule that had to be opposed by anyone wanting to develop progressive alternatives to capitalism, as opposed to the particularly reductive notion of socialism on offer in the eastern bloc.

The Prague Spring had a profound effect on the more thoughtful elements of the Western Left, convincing many of them that their own interests were at odds with Great Power politics generally. The suspension of debate concerning the aims and goals of socialism in favour of the quietistic acceptance of the Soviet Union's 'leading role', so prevalent among radical intellectuals in the earlier decades of the twentieth century, gave way to a new experimentalism and a desire to re-examine the terms and conditions of their radical commitments. This in turn led to a profusion of socialisms and socialist groups, each with its own idea of how the world should look, how it was to be brought about, and what structures were needed to ensure participation. Even the communist movement itself, hitherto silent on the question of the Soviet Union's credibility as a progressive force, fractured into various official and unofficial splinters. Discounting the various Maoisms thrown up as an ultra-radical response to the crisis of communism, the most significant of these currents coalesced around the label 'Eurocommunism'. Some of the concerns and themes of this fracturing of the left in the wake of 1968 have a resonance that can be heard in contemporary debates over the future of anti-capitalism. These include:

- The idea of the *death of the working class* as the agent of radical change. Sociologically, western society was, according to many, becoming 'post-industrial' or post-Fordist. The old industries that created the strong ties of identity amongst the working class were dying off, to be replaced by service industries or unemployment – neither of which provided the basis for class solidarity and collective action. If radical politics had any future it was in response to the rise of 'post-materialist' values in the young and socially marginalised, both groups prominent in the events in Paris and Prague.
- Reflecting the above, *identity* was becoming a factor in disunity. People were more ready to identify with sub-groups

and sub-lifestyles rather than with larger aggregates such as 'the working class'. It was said that people now saw themselves as part of some or other 'minority'. Accordingly mobilisation could not be effected in and through conventional mechanisms, particularly via the mass party, but had to take account of the differing needs and perceptions of minority groups.

- Post-capitalist schemas could only work on the basis of the acceptance of plurality and diversity. This led to much fashionable talk of the need to recognise the necessity for 'civil society', human rights and the opening of the sphere of democracy to new groups and new forms of representation. The seizure of state power on the Bolshevik model was firmly displaced in favour of a variety of strategies including, where pertinent, electoral participation, lobbying and direct action.

In the wake of 1968 'The Left' rapidly dissipated into various currents, some radical and transformative, others much less so. The fracturing of the left hardly looks helpful from the point of view of the mobilisation of people behind an ideal that could challenge and in turn supplant capitalism. Yet what it tacitly signalled was the *complexity* of thinking the post-capitalist 'after' and thus the necessity for a generally more open, more tolerant kind of politics so that different voices, minorities and interests could be heard. In short the perceived failure of Soviet communism opened a space for dialogue and for the appearance of a multitude of diverse, plural and, it has to be said, conflicting accounts of how post-capitalism was to be pursued. The Prague Spring was in its own way an ideological Pandora's Box, out of which sprang a variety of radicalisms, socialisms and humanisms. The dream of a communist Front uniting the Eastern Left and the Western Left lay in tatters. The dream was in any case no more than a nightmare. Its dissipation was the necessary prelude to a fundamental reconsideration of the manner by which progressive politics could be advanced.

Paris '68: unofficial politics and the new radicalism

Such developments were further underlined by the tumultuous events in Paris that same spring. Rather like Seattle itself, the shape of French political life was radically transformed in a matter of hours by the efforts of an initially small number of university students led by an even smaller coterie of tutors, intellectuals and ideological outcasts, including some of the most celebrated (or notorious) figures of the theoretical, ideological and political rea-lignment that followed '68 such as Jean-François Lyotard. Protesting against the iniquities of university funding (in particu-lar the closing of the Nanterre campus), the protests quickly radicalised and generalised into an outright rejection of the French political and cultural establishment, and even more gen-erally into a rejection of the materialist values and way of life that seemed to have stultified French life. All around Paris the now familiar slogans and images of outright rebellion could be seen: 'Be Realistic: Demand the Impossible'; 'Choose Life'; 'It is Forbidden to Forbid'; 'Take your Desires for Reality'. The stu-dent protests quickly descended into a general paralysis of Parisian life as they were joined by workers at the huge Renault plants on the outskirts of the city. For a brief moment, something like a re-enactment of the 1871 Paris Commune seemed possible, together with a complete breakdown of the French state. De Gaulle and the French elites were caught completely una-wares, with the result that the strikes spread like wildfire, paralys-ing French economic and political life for a matter of weeks. It seemed for a fleeting moment that literally anything had become possible, including the 'impossible'. However, through a combina-tion of political bullying and cautious trade union leadership, the crisis passed, leaving a bitter legacy that still excites the French political classes on both sides of the ideological divide. How though does all of this have a bearing on the issues under review?

Paris '68 is significant for a number of reasons. The first and most obvious is that it represented the first real upsurge of 'unofficial' politics in post-war western Europe. What became obvious in the unfolding of the events was that the French Communist Party (PCF), hitherto the focus for anti-capitalist demands in France, had become an irrelevance from the point of view both of the uprising itself, and the demands and politics that it represented. The PCF seemed part of the problem, not part of the solution. According to its critics, the PCF was a large, unwieldy and utterly bureaucratised mainstream party that seemed content merely to act out its anointed role as oppositional counter-weight to the centre and right. In this sense it had become part of the political establishment, and as far distant from the concerns of the young as any other party. Its tired narrative of factory-based struggles, heroic sacrifices and command planning was by-passed by a much more anarchic, spontaneous and free-flowing discourse of liberation from the suffocating weight of all inherited 'roles', whether they be based on 'class', 'ideology' or any other pre-packaged formula. In this sense the dominant credo of '68 was hardly Marxist in the orthodox sense of the term at all, but more nearly 'situationist', after the Situationist International.

Formed earlier in the late 1950s by avowedly *ex*-Marxist (in the official sense) figures such as Guy Debord and Raoul Vaneigem, the Situationists offered an original mix of Sartrean existentialism, Dada-inspired surrealism and a loose-limbed variant of historical materialism that focused on the corrosive effects of the consumer society on personal and collective autonomy. What they proposed was an aesthetic break-out from conformity to roles, to stereotypes, political parties, majoritarianism, and the mainstream. In their view, capitalism had to be resisted not only at the level of the political, of institutions and structures of power, but also at the level of the personal, of the subject of politics, of his or her *desires*. From this position emerged a novel strategy of resistance based, not upon the revolutionary seizure of power, but upon a process by which capitalism would be *subverted from within* as a prelude to its displacement by other ways of living. How was this to be achieved? Two themes are important for the purposes of considering the relevance of these ideas for contemporary anti-capitalism: the idea of the *détournement* of the capitalist aesthetic and thus the capitalist structure of desire; and the idea of the 'spectacle' as a medium for eliciting resistance as well as compliance.

Détournement, the 'spectacle' and contemporary anti-capitalism

Taking *détournement* first, the idea was that through a subtle juxtaposition or alteration of capitalist 'signs' we would be compelled to reflect on the authenticity of the need for whatever it was that was being offered as a satisfier of our desires. This could be a simple gesture such as drawing a moustache on the image of a desirable woman being used to sell perfume. This would in turn subvert the message we are supposed to glean from the ad: wearing this perfume will make one as glamorous as the woman in the picture. Advertising could be defaced, scribbled on, reworded, all in the name of producing a moment's reflection on the part of the observer, but reflection (so it was hoped) not just on the commodity value of the thing being sold, but on the nature of 'commodity fetishism', the manner by which objects are imbued with apparently magical, sexual or otherwise heightened properties for the purpose of making them more desirable to the consumer. *Détournement* has now become a central pillar of anti-capitalist resistance the world over, though the terms 'subvertising' and 'guerrilla advertising' are more familiar. *Adbusters*, the collective that produces the slickly produced journal of the same name, deploys the Situationist strategy of *détournement*, using digital techniques to mask or overcode advertising, as well as chronicling the efforts of the many groups involved in 're-facing' billboards in the US. As Naomi Klein documents in

No Logo, subvertising is a key strategy, particularly in the US, in the war against the commodification of life, aimed at corporate power and the penetration of logos, brands and advertising into hitherto sheltered domains of existence such as schools and libraries. As is evident, 'culture jamming' is a direct inheritance of the situationist understanding of political resistance as one based on a struggle at the level of 'the everyday' for the hearts and minds of the denizens of advanced industrial society.

The same is true for the notion of the spectacle as a key plank of resistance countering capitalist commodification. To the Situationists, capitalism is a highly visual aesthetic: it seeks to retain our interest, make us aware of brands, logos, shopping malls, publicity, so that we will buy more. A resistance that fails to engage with capitalism in the visual and emotional field will thus fail to challenge the stranglehold it exercises over our sense of who and what we are. A fundamental disruption thus has to be effected in front of us, indeed within us. Resistance was regarded to be not just about power, about storming offices and throwing out the ruling class, but also about changing our view of the world both literally and metaphorically. Nor could resistance be a quietistic or theory driven exercise; it had to be a counter-spectacle, an alternative aesthetic experience. Like the concept of *détournement*, the idea of the spectacle has been taken up and accounts at least in part for one of the most interesting facets of anti-capitalist protests, which is that of the quite self-conscious attempt to capture the feel of a carnival or circus. There is noise, music, masks, colour, drama, costumes, theatre, giant sculpture. It could be argued that this emphasis on the aesthetic dimension of protest reaches further back still, to the medieval carnivals that toured the market towns and villages of Europe. It is also suggestive of the carnivals of the peasants and landless poor across the developing world, each regarded with dread by governing elites. A carnival doesn't have leaders. It doesn't have a manifesto or programme. It is not in this sense outwardly threatening, but instead represents a break from the everyday business of working, earning, consuming, obeying. It creates uncertainty and excitement, unpredictability and contingency. It creates a sense of collective pleasure unconstrained by normality. The idea of carnival as a basis for resistance was one of the great rediscoveries of 1968 and lives on today in the strategy and outlook of anti-capitalist groupings such as Reclaim the Streets, *Ya Basta!* and the Occupy movement.

More generally, such developments portend the sense in which traditional revolutionary strategies which focused on the capturing of state power through storming government offices were challenged in significant ways, as too were the traditional means by which the 'masses' were to be mobilised. It was no longer enough to shout slogans through a loudhailer to effect a change in the way people thought about themselves. Nor could a mobilisation be effected through bureaucratic and unwieldy party machines. People would somehow have to divest themselves of their emotional investment in commodities, and more generally in capitalism, *in order to make* capitalism collapse. They needed to *desire* radical change before radical change became a possibility. A politics that ignored the place of desire could on this reading only repeat the mistakes of earlier revolutionaries. Such a politics was of necessity unofficial in scope and character. It was a politics of guerrilla tactics, of *détournement*, of aesthetic and subjective rebellion. It was, in the memorable phrase of the period, about making oneself a 'revolutionary of everyday life'. Such sentiments were to become increasingly prevalent in the run-up to Seattle and the emergence of the mobile carnival of resistance that was to become such a central feature of contemporary radical politics.

1968, 'new social movements' and direct action

Lest it be forgotten, 1968 was a momentous year more generally for the emergence of unofficial politics. This had two aspects.

The first as a *mobilisation against war*, and the second as a *mobilisation against the exclusion of women, minorities, groups and issues* hitherto overlooked or disregarded by mainstream or official politics. The Vietnam War and the Civil Rights Movement both initiated an unprecedented degree of mobilisation in the US and Europe, one with important lessons for today. Both the War and Civil Rights activism engaged and mobilised ordinary people in a manner without precedent in US politics, in turn serving to radicalise a generation of activists. What it showed in particular was that a mass mobilisation could be effected against an injustice rather than for some ideologically delineated vision. This is to say that *injustice* could be just as effective, if not more so, in terms of uniting people and encouraging them to reflect on the nature and circumstances of the power behind the injustice. It also demonstrated the utility of *direct action* as opposed to voting or standing for office. Direct action worked in the sense that in a televisual age, the image of thousands of young people protesting against lines of soldiers, placing flowers in their guns, chanting and singing for peace, was an important signal that a significant element of the population would not accept the legitimacy of the War without resistance. Nor, increasingly, would people accept the sight of Afro-Americans being beaten by the police for demanding nothing more than equality with their white peers. Fear of mobilisation has since the dawn of liberal-democracy been a powerful catalyst for changing politicians' minds, particularly those concerned for their electoral prospects. There is nothing like the sight of 'mobs' and 'crowds' to unsettle politicians who in general much prefer the docility of elections and parliamentary debate. From this point of view the mobilisations were significant in the decision of the US administration to pull out of Vietnam, as it finally did in 1973.

It was at least in part the experience of the anti-war movement that encouraged the growth of unofficial politics in the immediate aftermath of 1968. The most prominent initiative was the development of the women's movement across the advanced industrial world, and in later decades across the developing world too. Ironically, the growth of the women's movement was partly in response to the negative experience of women in the anti-war protests and to shared feelings of being excluded in the unstructured decision-making that underpinned the anti-war mobilisation. Like the anti-war movement, however, the effectiveness of the movement was largely framed in terms of its being *against* something that to most progressively minded individuals was clearly unjust, namely the deep inequality and voicelessness experienced by women across the world. And again, the remedy was often various forms of direct action ranging from demonstrations and sit-ins, to the invasion of the Miss World contest and the disruption of UK parliamentary proceedings and TV news broadcasts. Across the industrialised world, and in the developing world too, women organised themselves at work and in the public sphere, challenging the deep-seated inequalities and discriminations – some subtle, others much less so – that permeated the fabric of 'patriarchal' societies. They also experimented with forms of organisation and action that were to become staples of the anti-capitalist protests. Indeed the idea of extreme decentralisation and horizontally organised networks of like-minded groupings was something of a template for the more radically orientated direct action groupings that currently abound.

The growth of the women's movement as an unofficial form of politics was later matched by the dramatic emergence of the environmental movement in the 1970s and 1980s. This was 'fuelled' in particular by the Oil Crisis of 1973, which jolted people into considering the prospect that the world's resources were not in fact unlimited as had hitherto seemed to have been assumed. United around the theme of the need to move from unsustainable growth to sustainable development, the environmental movement was one of the first to generate a significant number of Non-Governmental Organisations (NGOs) such as Friends of the Earth and Greenpeace (both founded in 1971). The significance of such

groupings is firstly that they gave an alternative outlet for concerned or politicised individuals who had become alienated or
turned off by mainstream politics. They were often highly professional, tightly focused, and well funded with clear, practical and
non-ideologically driven purposes in mind. In a sense such groups
were political innocents, and this was part of their attraction for
those wearied by the utilitarian politicking of official parties.
Nothing seemed to be hidden; there was no secret agenda and
there were few hangers-on or cronies who had to be paid for out
of hard-earned subscriptions and donations. Concerned individuals could support such causes without a sense that they were tiny
cogs in some much larger power-seeking machine.

Some of these preconceptions are no doubt naïve when
transferred to today's equivalents. Many NGOs would make the
efforts of many minor or smaller parties look thoroughly ama-
teurish by comparison. But this is hardly the point. What *seemed*
important then and still seems important now is that such groups
are idealistic without being ideological, they are campaigning
without being cynical; they are active not passive, which is to say
they are often the fulcrum for direct action and thus direct
involvement by their members. They *do* something, rather than
waiting for things to happen as often appears to be the case with
political parties ('just wait until *we* get into power'). This contrast
between the active and idealistic green movements and the reactive and pragmatic political establishment was at its sharpest at
the Rio Earth Summit in 1992, in retrospect something akin to
a rehearsal for the later protests. Within the conference centres
the rows of bemused, suited figures peddling modest proposals
for reductions in emissions, saving forests, oceans and endangered
species. Outside was a blur of colour, noise and vibrancy with
myriad groups jostling for the attentions of the world's media,
calling for radical change, wholesale transformation, and the end
of an unsustainable free market capitalism. How familiar all this
would become after Seattle.

The women's movement and the environmental movements were by no means the only significant new social movements to emerge in the reshaping of the political landscape after 1968. They were to be joined by an astonishing array of what are termed *single-issue groups* many of which were to become significant presences on the anti-capitalist circuit. Chief amongst these were groups campaigning on the basis of an enlargement of the sphere of rights, which over the course of the last third of the twentieth century became the dominant discourse of unofficial politics, particularly in the US. There were groups campaigning for *animal rights*, for various *human rights* particularly those focusing on gay rights, and the rights of ethnic and racial minorities to equal treatment or to 'affirmative action'. There were campaigns for the *rights of workers* in the developing world and the rights of workers in the developed world whose livelihoods were threatened by the liberalisation of the global market. There were groups campaigning for the right to immigrate, the right to health-care or drug treatments. One of the largest mobilisations in recent years was in support of those who had contracted AIDS/HIV. Vast demonstrations were held, as well as telethons, sit-ins, and petitions accusing the political establishment of inaction. By the end of the 1990s it seemed that the clamour of unofficial politics was almost overwhelming. And yet still the experts and commentators talked of the boredom and apathy of the 'ordinary person on the street', equating the growing reluctance of young people in particular to mandate politicians as a sign that they were somehow uninterested in politics. After Seattle there would be noticeably fewer such generalisations.

By the time of the fall of the Berlin Wall in 1989 we can already see in outline the elements shaping a new kind of oppositional politics. Its characteristics were the following:

* *It was ideologically and politically diverse.* The decline in communism, and indeed social democracy, was not matched

by the emergence of a new hegemonic idea – a new ideology that could claim to represent or embody the hopes and aspirations of those who were not accommodated within the liberal-democratic consensus. There were myriad ideologies, narratives of liberation, collective demands. But there were also those motivated by *specific injustices* as opposed to the desire to create a just world. This is to say there was an activism driven by non-ideological *as well as* ideological concerns. Those who protested against the abuse of animals in testing could just as well be motivated by the simple love of animals as by the desire to create a world in which the abuse of animals was in some moral or political sense impossible.

- *It was organisationally diverse.* As the account above illustrates some groups such as the NGOs and charities were formally constituted professional or semi-professional organisations with permanent staffs and offices geared up for lobbying politicians and corporations, some of them with turnovers of many millions, large subscriber bases, glossy brochures and magazines. They could be bureaucratically organised with clear hierarchies, leaderships and professional accounting procedures. At the other end of the scale were groups constituted informally, meeting sporadically, with little of the paraphernalia of the professional lobbyists. They could be 'one event wonders', or loosely co-ordinated with some particular purpose in view. Most groups were, however, anti-official politics, parties, elections. Even the NGOs kept themselves clear of the contaminating effects of 'big politics'. Unofficial politics remained over the period unofficial, which is to say that groups kept clear of electioneering for fear of becoming compromised by the realities of electoral politics. The major exception to this trend was the Greens who across the globe formed themselves into political parties as well as campaigning organisations. The pattern of success was, however, hardly uniform. In Germany the Greens made some breakthroughs and participated in the highest levels of government in recent German administrations – at the cost of a continuing feud between 'deep' Greens and 'light' Greens over the virtue of an electorally based strategy. Elsewhere the picture was less rosy, particularly where the electoral system worked against the emergence of minor parties, as in Britain and the US.

- *It was an active as opposed to passive style of politics.* The politics of the new social movements was above all about participation, not representation. One of the key themes of the politics that emerges out of 1968 is the notion of 'being heard', whether this being heard was in the form of consciousness-raising groups such as those found in feminist circles, or in terms of more general notions of interactivity and partici- pation as found particularly in those groups organised around the need for direct action. It was direct action by the *members* of the group, not by representatives.

So at one level at least Fukuyama was right – which was in his assertion that Soviet communism was in some definitive sense 'dead'. But the assumption that oppositional politics as such was dead was flawed. Oppositional politics, a politics that took issue with the simple contention that all was right with 'actually exist- ing liberal-democracy' had not gone away: far from it. As is clear, there was a vast proliferation of oppositions, some ideologically driven, others much less so; some motivated by one issue or by one set of issues, others by a more general opposition to the *status quo*. Some of these currents were radical and transformative in outlook; others could be satisfied by some legal or political reform that would remove a specific injustice. From this point of view it was easy for conservative commentators to conclude that the threat to the status quo had been met and defeated. There was no global movement, no force that opposed liberal-capitalism in the way that the Soviet Union and Communist Bloc had.

It was also easy for left-wing commentators to wring their hands and worry about the prospects for social change in the face of what seemed like a fragmentation of political energies, and progressive causes into distinct and separate campaigns. The political thought of the 1980s and 1990s is full of such remorse, and full of attempts to hang the blame for the fragmentation on some group or other. Jürgen Habermas, the great inheritor of the quasi-Marxist tradition of Critical Theory, famously accused French postmodern theorists of disarming the progressive or radical cause in their insistence on the relativity of truth and the impossibility of the reconstruction of the 'project of emancipa-tion' around some organising principle of the sort that commu-nism seemed to offer to an earlier generation. Others – not just French theorists – revelled in the sense of fragmentation for pre-cisely that reason, pointing out that the communist 'metanarra-tive' had been responsible for condemning millions to the Gulag. The fragmentation Habermas lamented was nothing less than the effect of the thawing of the monolithic emancipatory story, releasing voices, causes and injustices that had previously been subject to the overarching logic of the communist project. 'Plurality' and 'fragmentation' were in this sense two sides of the same coin. One person's diversity was another person's loss of focus and dissipated radical energies.

If they did not quite resolve the matter, then the Seattle pro-tests in 1999 at least gave a glimpse of the possibility both sets of commentators had arguably discounted, namely the emergence of a movement that was *both* diverse *and* radical, both 'fragmented' and 'united' in its common cause. The remaining question for this chapter is: how do we get from this picture of plurality and frag-mentation to a global anti-capitalist movement? What changed after 1989?

Global anti-capitalism and the challenge to neoliberalism

Two themes are immediately pertinent here, both linked by the theme of communication. The first is that in some important sense diverse groups began to identify a *common enemy*. Leading on from this, was the possibility for a kind of *global dialogue* of the oppressed, or the 99% as the Occupy movement would later put it. That enemy was neoliberalism (or 'corporate power' or 'transnational capitalism' – all fingers pointing at the same target). The second point is that they exploited opportunities to communicate with each other. Here the story is one of *capacity*, of the harnessing of new technologies for the ends of common political protest. How does this pan out?

Neoliberalism in the sights

As regards the *common enemy*, the period immediately following 1989 saw neoliberalism break out of the narrower domestic agendas to which it had hitherto been tied. Reagan and Thatcher were both tireless *neoliberals* in their own way, but they were isolated in a sea of social democratic, welfarist and quasi-collectivist systems. The world of 1989 was one where most governments were still committed to defending the post-war consensus. But with a general slowdown in the world economy, and the resultant unemployment and dwindling tax revenues, the consensus came under attack. Conservative administrations forged ahead with a fundamental restructuring, not only of their own economies, but also the trading regimes of which they were a part, all of course with the blessing of the World Bank, IMF and OECD. In 1994, for example, the US finally corralled Mexico and Canada into the North America Free Trade Area (NAFTA), allowing full penetration of corporations into hitherto untapped markets through the abolition of impediments to trade between those

within the free trade zone. In Europe the post–Maastricht negotiations focussed on the establishment of a single currency, bringing with it policies of fiscal rectitude, balanced budgets and cuts
in public expenditure. The 1990s were to be tough for labour,
with millions of public sector jobs dispensed with as previously
nationalised industries were led to the market, like so many pigs
for the slaughter. After a long period of retrenchment, trade
unions in advanced industrial countries polarised between those
who bought the rhetoric of 'There is no alternative' (TINA) and
those who decided attack was the best means of defence. Some
fell into line between political leaders who promised in a nation-
alistic vein that they would safeguard jobs at home. Others saw
what was coming, and renewed the idealistic and internationalist
credo of the labour movement. For those who had given up on
the labour movement as a source of opposition, the Seattle protests, which saw trade unionists turn out in force, surprised many
both within and outside activist circles. But Seattle was perhaps
also a premonition of things to come, with the main bulk of trade
unionists remaining on their official AFL–CIO march with more
militant unions such as the Steelworkers (USWA) and Longshore
Workers Union (ILWU) teamed up for the historic 'turtles and
teamsters' protest that grabbed the headlines.

By the end of the 1990s neoliberal policies had become more
or less ubiquitous. Even countries with a seemingly unwavering
commitment to collectivist policies such as France rapidly
succumbed. Lionel Jospin, the ex-Trotskyite leader of the *Parti
Socialiste*, ushered in a new era of austerity in France. It might
have suited his dour character, but not the supporters of
Mitterrand's once fiercely collectivist party who turned against
him in the 2002 presidential elections. Elsewhere there seemed a
genuine chance that the nascent global market would collapse
under the weight of its own liquidity. First Asia, then Russia, then
South America buckled under the difficulty of maintaining political control over economic systems that, now fully open to the

vagaries of speculative capital, seemed beyond the capacity of politicians to control. The sheer scale of the misery that accompanied the wild gyrations of the global economy is difficult for many of us to comprehend. What is less difficult to comprehend is the feeling of profound resentment that such conditions engendered in those who suffered as a result. If history teaches anything of relevance to our subject, it is that conditions of economic crisis can be expected to lead to political radicalisation and the search for far-reaching answers to deep-seated problems. The impetus to the development of anti-capitalist ideas and initiatives was ultimately propelled by the very factors that so many western radicals had come to discount in their preference for a 'post-materialist' analysis: poverty, unemployment and powerlessness. What was perhaps notable was that economic crisis was not confined to the global poor. Formerly wealthy countries felt the effects as much as their impoverished neighbours, and all compounded by an increasing sense that only a genuinely global effort could get at the cause of the collective misery.

By the end of the 2000s, then, the 'end of history' thesis looked tired to the point of exhaustion. What it discounted was the impact of crisis, recession, unemployment and diminishing demand. There was very little triumphalism in the wake of the GFC which began to take grip on global affairs from 2007 onwards. Initially a banking crisis, as we have seen, the GFC rapidly turned into a 'credit crunch' that only major intervention by nation-states could prevent from spiralling out of control. The cure was however almost as painful as the affliction itself. Under pressure from international organisations and local elites, states chose to bail out local banks and financial bodies, but at a heavy cost to their own balance sheets. By the end of the 2000s many states found themselves in deep financial difficulty and in danger of going bust themselves. Iceland, not previously noted for profligacy, went bankrupt. Small European economies started to suffer as 'deleveraging' or the reduction of debt by banks as well as states made the costs of borrowing rise in dramatic terms. Ireland, Portugal, Greece and Spain were compelled by the EU and the IMF to slash public spending and implement 'austerity' measures that would help balance the books after the credit fuelled boom. Large economies such as the UK embarked on slash and burn measures to cut public spending. TINA reappeared, only this time as an excuse for cutting back on state expenditure, a set of measures memorably encapsulated by Naomi Klein in her phrase and book of the same name, 'the shock doctrine'. In the US debt mounted as quantitative easing poured into the economy to prop up ailing banks and industries. The only sector of the economy that seemed to be doing well from these measures was that of the bankers and bosses themselves, many of whom celebrated their successful lobbying with further multi-million-dollar bonuses and salary increases.

It was, so it seems, the ugly self-contradictions inherent in this behaviour that inspired a new wave of anti-capitalist militancy and activism. In Spain, groups inspired by the Arab Spring mobilised as the *Indignados* (the indignant) to protest against the austerity measures and call for 'true democracy'. In the UK disaffiliated movements and currents such as UK Uncut targeted banks and companies associated with the tax-avoiding 'off shore' economy using situationist tactics of direct action, occupation and carnival. In the US a regular protest in the heart of Wall Street became an occupation, which spread like wildfire across the country and abroad to become the Occupy movement. Many if not all of these initiatives were expressly anti-capitalist in outlook even if they rejected much of the heritage of radical politics: the rhetoric of building the party, the organising of revolution, the planning of a post-capitalist after. These were movements and initiatives that represented continuity rather than change from the atmosphere of Seattle, the Zapatista Uprising and the World Social Forum: 'One No, Many Yeses'. Infuriating for some; inspirational for others.

The technological great leap forward: the social technology explosion

As regards the *capacity* of activists to organise and cross-pollinate, then the arrival of and access to advanced communications technology must be regarded as of crucial significance. Indeed, the combination of the internet with social technology such as Twitter and Facebook has to be regarded as the most astonishing boon for activism of any technology since the arrival of the printing press or perhaps the typewriter. How did these technologies come to assume such importance? They:

- give visibility and presence to otherwise marginal groups;
- facilitate the creation of activist networks;
- allow greater co-ordination of activity;
- provide alternative sources of information and news;
- offer new ways of organising and instigating direct action ('hacktivism'; 'Net war').

Firstly and most obviously, the internet gives *visibility* and *presence* to groups and causes that would otherwise remain hidden from view. Before the internet, political groups relied on paper for the dissemination of their views. In the era of cheap paper and photocopiers it is not that expensive to produce leaflets, pamphlets and posters. The problem is trying to put them in places where target audiences can find them. Many booksellers and news agents are loathe to give space to such materials on commercial and ideological grounds. Numerous cases were taken out against commercial retailers for precisely these reasons in the 1970s and 1980s. Until very recently the job was done by radical and alternative bookshops or cafes usually located in major towns and cities, and some of them survive and prosper to great effect. However, with the internet, virtually every radical or oppositional current had its presence on the web. Anyone with access could download articles or back issues of a journal, and get a sense of philosophy or stance towards the great matters of the day. Moreover, the internet promotes a crude form of equality between groups. Type 'anarchy' into a search engine and we are presented with the URL addresses of tiny bed-sit operations as well as large or well-organised groups. This can be a strength as well as a weakness in organisational terms (as we shall see); but in terms of *visibility* it transforms the potential of groups to be seen and heard.

Secondly, the internet preserved the particularity of distinct groups and causes whilst greatly facilitating the creation of *networks* of the like-minded. Groups could make common cause with other groups that shared their values, beliefs doctrine, priorities or purposes. This could be achieved either through a simple links page which indicates which groups they felt some sense of common cause with, or through more elaborate networks, sites and mechanisms that acted as umbrella organisations all of their own. By the end of the 1990s networks such as the Independent Media Network ('Indymedia'), People's Global Action, Global Exchange and Zmag.org were encouraging an exchange of news and views amongst activists, offering message boards, calendars of meetings and protests, contact addresses. But the significance of virtual networks and exchanges such as these went well beyond the obvious point that they permitted a flow of useful information concerning the whereabouts of protests and demonstrations. They fostered a form of interaction that preserved the integrity and autonomy of the constituent parts. No group was subject to the will of another. No group had to recognise one as a leading group or as the 'vanguard' of the movement. There was no need for bureaucracy, permanent staffs, officials, leadership, or even premises, beyond somewhere to house a server. Here was a form of interaction that denied the need for the very institutional and logistical framework that had for a century defined the terms and conditions of political activism.

It enacted a form of electronic anarchy, an apparent free-for-all in which anyone with access to the necessary equipment could make their presence felt. The internet encouraged a version of the commons to come to life, a space/place that was largely ungoverned and ungovernable either by corporate interests or by would-be revolutionary leaders and parties. Governments and corporations could watch and spy on internet activists, but they couldn't control or eliminate them.

Thirdly, the internet and social media permitted the *co-ordination of activity* along the above lines. This is to say that activists now had a means of marshalling activism along the same anarchistic lines that underpinned the growth of the internet itself. One group could alert many other groups to the existence of a movement of nuclear waste, to the shutting of a factory, to the destruction of an ecologically sensitive site, to the arrival of US military personnel. It could suggest a time, place and appropriate form of direct action. It could smooth the activist task and give a sense of solidarity to those who might otherwise wonder what awaited. It made activism logistically easier, if not less risky. As social technologies moved on, so static message boards gave way to more dynamic and interactive forms of communication to mobilise people, in turn changing the nature of the actions that could be organised. UK Uncut, to take one example, deployed social media to considerable effect, largely by-passing the usual trappings of radical activism. Focusing on protesting against tax-avoiding UK corporations, local groups nominated a shop to occupy, sent out messages via Twitter giving details of time and place, and waited for sympathisers to turn up. And turn up they did. Part of the attraction of such actions is that none of these arrangements are binding in the sense that they prevent a given group or individual from conducting his or her own form of protest. They don't require membership fees, loyalty to a manifesto or programme, long evenings spent with tiresome ideologues reading obscure works of political economy. The emphasis is on forms of collective action, but without at the same time reducing the individuality or autonomy of the constituent elements. Social media fostered a new style or mode of activism that promoted direct and immediate kinds of protest whilst preserving the singularity of the actors themselves.

Fourthly, the internet offers an alternative source of news and information. In an era where media ownership has progressively narrowed to a handful of mega-conglomerates, the internet provides a vital alternative perspective on global events. As print media becomes ever more dumbed-down in the hunt for the lowest common denominator, internet-based news gathering, the sharing of informal news and reporting becomes ever more important, not just to activists, but to anyone wanting an alternative take on global events and developments. But it is not just the content that is important, it is also the speed with which events can be narrated and relayed to networks of activists and those more generally concerned about global politics. The level of information and analysis may be uneven; but the ability of otherwise voiceless groups and minorities to interact with a global audience has been one of the keys to the development of the new radicalism. It has increased the awareness of groups concerning each other and permitted the exchange of stories, strategies, tactics in mutual solidarity.

Finally, one of the most commented upon aspects of the growth of the internet has been the growth of *internet-based direct action* as a supplement to more conventional forms of protesting. In a twist on the subvertising theme discussed above, the websites of corporations and government agencies have been attacked, with home pages altered in judicious ways to subvert the official 'welcome'. Even the CIA's website has suffered from the attentions of the hacktivists despite their preoccupation with security in the era of Net war. There have been episodes of 'cyber-squatting' in which hackers have occupied the servers of target organisations, refusing to 'move' until they have been heard.

We can also mention the practice of 'pinging', where servers are attacked by message auto-replies that swamp the home server. Such activities, once associated with university students working apart from wider protest movements, have increasingly adopted a collective character through 'Anonymous' the catch-all term for those who identify with hacktivism as a form of protest. Paradoxically, Anonymous became more 'visible' through the adoption of the Guy Fawkes mask that made frequent appearances at Occupy and the protests of the *Indignados*. More generally, where once hacktivism implied an individual form of resistance, it has increasingly taken on a more collective form, washing in and out of various struggles and resistances in the name of the commons.

Conclusion

So oppositional politics did not go away in the manner predicted by Fukuyama and the ideologues of liberal capitalism. It went underground. But what is interesting is the way in which the underground itself changed in radical ways in a short space of time. Underground no longer meant 'hidden from view', 'without the means of communication' or 'isolated'. Underground now implied a network of interactivity, hidden from the daily newshounds, but nonetheless resurgent and in the cases of groups in the developing world insurgent. Certain events, like the Zapatista uprising, Seattle, the inaugural World Social Forum and the emergence of Occupy, make the rest of the world aware of the scope and extensiveness of these networks. But the emergence of social technologies such as the internet and Twitter has also highlighted for the activists themselves the idea that a network-based activism could be something more than a gesture of solidarity for otherwise disparate struggles. Over the past two decades there has been a remarkable change in the mindset and strategy of those who engage in protest and resistance. Something snowballed and it was not just the sense or scope of the protests themselves. Activists and commentators began to take seriously the idea of a global anti-capitalist movement – or, less dramatically, 'global civil society'. On the other hand it was easy to see what the clamour of activity was against: neoliberalism, the 1%, corporate domination of the planet. What was more difficult to get a handle on was what such a movement was *for*. Was the movement really to be a movement, or a vast structure of connected and interconnected groups and causes? Was it to have a wider agenda or programme which it could offer as an alternative to contemporary capitalism? Curious to say, with the re-emergence of radical activism the easy part was over. An anti-capitalist ethic and mode of resistance had been reignited the world over. But where was it going?

3

A 'movement of movements' I : 'reformism', or 'globalisation with a human face'

At the end of the last chapter we noted that in the wake of the protests against the meeting of the WTO in Seattle, it became customary to speak in terms of the existence of an anti-capitalist – or sometimes anti-globalisation – movement. Yet there are many difficulties in getting to grips with the nature of a movement that seemed to many to appear from nowhere. One of the immediate problems is how to delineate anti-capitalism itself. Do we start thinking in terms of all those who are or have been present at various protests and carnivals where anti-capitalists meet? In other words, do we try to define anti-capitalism primarily by reference to distinct *events*, examining in sociological style the various presences at Seattle, in the Occupy movement, or the Greek protests? Or, do we think more in terms of the *ideas* of those who describe themselves as anti-capitalist or who in some other way associate themselves with radical struggles, for example by participating at the World Social Forums, by demonstrating in support of the landless peasants of Brazil or the sweatshop workers of South-East Asia?

As is clear, the two overlap to a certain extent in the sense that many of those who turn up to protests, and consider themselves activists, are at the same time those whose animosity to capitalism is driven by certain ideas about how the world should look. But not everyone who turns up to anti-capitalist protests is 'anti-capitalist' in this sense, and quite a lot are not. One should never discount those who have bunked off school for a day, *agents provocateurs*, free loaders, the curious, sensation-seekers, indeed sociologists and academics studying contemporary protests. Some change their minds because of what they hear at the protests. Some in other words may arrive at a protest as a representative of a trade union or as a single issue activist and become committed to a more radical position because they have become convinced that the best way of advancing trade union causes or confronting specific injustices is to oppose corporate or neoliberal capitalism. Protests, marches and demonstrations have never in this sense been mere passive aggregates of individuals, but are also moments when people learn about the grievances and beliefs of others. Indeed if the anti-capitalist phenomenon can be credited with one thing it is this very evidently *educative* function that meetings and protests have performed. A lot of people have learned an awful lot about the condition of other people, and in turn have learned to see themselves and their apparently discrete causes as merely part of a more general problematic. On the other hand, what is also evident is that many people who consider themselves anti-capitalist in some general way do not take part in the various anti-capitalist protests. This includes many who are too poor to travel, those who are compelled to work on a particular day in question, those who for some reason cannot face crowds or potentially violent gatherings, those in prison, those with child-care responsibilities or some other commitment that keeps them away. 'Anti-capitalism' must in this sense be more than the spectacle. It must be about ideas. Without ideas there can be no event. More seriously, without ideas there can be no debate on the 'after' of capitalism. Ultimately if we want to understand anti-capitalism we need to understand what it is that anti-capitalism is as a set of *ideas*.

Even if we accept that what we should be looking at are anti-capitalist ideas, further problems follow, for what is even more evident is the degree to which anti-capitalism is a mere umbrella term for myriad causes, ideologies, movements, groups and world views. It is for this reason that many who try to describe the nature of anti-capitalism now tend to use the term 'movement of movements'. Anti-capitalism lacks many of the characteristics that defined movements of the past. In particular it lacks a unifying ideology or programme. There are no holy books, no doctrine or philosophy to which one can refer to get a sense of a core orientation. Nor is there a leader, considered in charismatic, doctrinal or organisational terms. There are certainly important, even iconic, figures. We could mention here Subcomandante Marcos of the Zapatistas, and public intellectuals such as Noam Chomsky, Slavoj Žižek and Naomi Klein. There are also leaders of national movements and governments who would also be considered figures associated with the broad struggle against neoliberalism, such as Hugo Chavez and Evo Morales. But as is clear from recent initiatives there is a quite general hostility to the traditional leader figure and a determination to ensure that one does not emerge. Occupy doesn't have leaders, nor do the *Indignados* or the various currents opposing austerity measures in countries such as Greece. Today's anti-capitalists do not lack leadership – they actively *oppose* it insofar as that implies coalescence around the analysis, needs or personality of a single individual.

It follows that if we wish to understand today's anti-capitalism then we have to accept the central fact about it, namely that it is composed of *disaggregated, plural and competing conceptions* of how capitalism is to be combated and changed. Indeed anti-capitalism is defined as much by the *differences* between the various elements composing the movement of movements as by any *similarities*. To say it is a movement of movements is to say that it is composed of distinct groupings or molecules, each with its own agenda, passions and constituency. Whether a movement can be *effective* on these terms is a question to which we will need to return. All we need note here is that up to the present theorists of resistance have assumed that there is a necessary correlation between the unity of political purpose of a movement and its effectiveness. Without a certain agreement on ends and means, there is no movement as such, only an umbrella beneath which otherwise irreconcilable causes and groups may temporarily shelter before moving on down their own separate paths. It follows from the above that in order to get a sense of anti-capitalism today we need to get a sense of the nature of numerous discrete currents, what it is they offer in terms of an analysis of the present state of the world and in terms of a prescription for the future state of the world. Who are the anti-capitalists?

Analysing anti-capitalist ideas: beginnings

In attempting to think about the ideological commitments of a heterogeneous movement of this kind there is considerable temptation to reach for a rather tired tool of comparative political analysis, the left–right spectrum. This is to say that we think in terms of a one-dimensional plane with 'radical' at one end and 'reformers' at the other. We then plot the various tendencies of the movement on the plane and in such fashion depict the differences in ideology and strategy along it. There is a certain sense in which this has a validity here, but only a certain sense. Looking at the anti-capitalist movement in disaggregated terms we do indeed see very radical groups, less radical groups and not very radical groups, all in the same political space. So much will be obvious to anyone who has been privy to the efforts of anti-capitalists to agree on a programme for change. The left–right spectrum is, however, too simplistic for our purposes. What it leaves out is just as important as what is left in, which is the fact that many groupings within the anti-capitalist movement are evidently either *non-ideological* or *post-ideological*. This is to say that there are groupings that are quite explicitly opposed to the idea that what the movement needs is an alternative vision of how the world should look. For them, opposition to capitalism, or neoliberalism, stems from the fact that capitalism imposes a vision of the world thereby making impossible other forms of life, other ways of living, other kinds of social interaction, other ways of organising communities. Initiatives such as Occupy and the *Indignados* have this character. They are against the '1%' dictating how we should live – which still leaves open the question of how we should or might live. This, one feels, is not the point of the action. Rather the point is to accentuate how a tiny elite dictates our political, social and economic existence. Being dictated to is wrong: it is not what democracy is supposed to look like. Indigenous forms of resistance often have a similar aspect to them. They wish to be left alone rather than to be incorporated into some narrative of development, human rights or collective betterment.

All this is by contrast to *ideologically-driven* groupings that historically have counter-posed the present to some ideal or, in any case, much better alternative. The great tendency of post-Enlightenment political thought has been of this nature. Starting from some account of human nature, human needs or wants, some conception of social progress of historical development, thinkers have generated a critique of the given states of affairs based on an an allegedly superior idea of how the world could look. In saying this, we should be clear that anti-capitalist ideas are no different to those of, for example, liberals. Poster figures for neoliberalism such as Friedrich Hayek and Milton

Friedman had a strong sense of where the world had gone wrong and what measures were needed to make it better. People need markets to express themselves and to help social reproduction. Thus the more 'market' we have the better. It is for this reason that we talk about neoliberalism. An 'ism' is a complete package. It contains an *analysis* of the present combined with a *prescription* for future happiness, well-being, progress.

As is clear, anti-capitalism is not like neoliberalism in this sense. There isn't one anti-capitalist ideology, but rather many anti-capitalisms. Not only are there various ideological currents, there are also forms of activism and different types of grouping that consciously reject ideology altogether. What is evident is that the anti-capitalist movement is composed *both* of radicals and reformists, and *also* composed of groups with strong ideological affiliations and identities and others that quite self-consciously

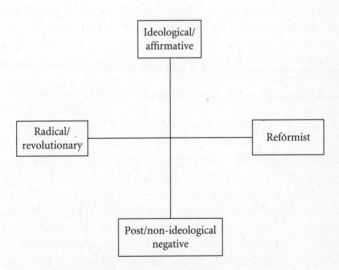

A two-dimensional typology of anti-capitalist positions

lack or reject such attachments. This suggests the need to dispense with a simple or horizontal left–right spectrum and instead to think in terms of a two-dimensional typology with a further vertical plane. We could then think in terms of a horizontal plane with the most radical groups at one end leading to the most reformist at the other. Then we cross-sect that plane with a vertical axis. On the vertical we could place ideological or affirmative groups closer to the top and non-/post-ideological groups near the bottom.

If all this sounds a little clinical and cut-dried, it is. The picture is actually much more complex, as will become apparent. Indeed one of the factors that cannot be represented diagrammatically is the presence of *single-issue groups, NGOs, and religious lobbyists*, many of which can hardly be described as anti-capitalist. However, a cross-sectional analysis at least gives us a *relatively* intelligible picture of the different ideological dimensions at work in the movement. It also gives us a sense of one or two important fault lines running across the movement, namely that between radicals and reformers, *and* that between groups whose opposition to capitalism stems from a prior ideological vantage point and those whose opposition stems from the desire to counter or negate an ideology, namely neoliberalism.

Over the next two chapters I will try to give a sense of how these affiliations operate in practice. In the next chapter we look at the radical wing of anti-capitalism. We begin, however, by looking at the reformist wing. I should make clear at this point that my interest in using the terms 'reformist' and 'radical' is merely as loose descriptors for different kinds of commitments. It is not my intention to imply that one position is implicitly or explicitly more valid than the other, though of course they *do* have this connotation in the infra-struggles of the anti-capitalist scene. For Marxists, reformists are people who invariably 'sell out' to capitalism. Yet reformist positions may well seem quite radical to those who have given little thought to the nature of global capitalism. This is only to be expected. Nonetheless what is meant by 'radical' here is a commitment to *a substantial or complete transformation of global capitalism*. Radicals *actually* want to rid the world of capitalism, which, as will be recalled from chapter 1, involves getting rid of the private ownership of the means of production, whether presided over by corporations or not. It stands for the abolition of production for profit and of the institution of wage labour. This, as will be apparent, is a tall order, some would say an impossibly utopian one, involving a complete or fundamental break with the present. Whether it would require a revolution in the sense of an overthrowing of the current global order is a very heated topic and one to which (again) we shall return in due course. Here, however, we discuss the ideas of those whose view of anti-capitalism falls short of the fundamental transformation called for by radical groups. They typically oppose *corporate* capitalism, but not capitalism as such. They are looking to break the spell of a particular kind of globalisation, namely the neoliberal variety, but are not ideologically or pragmatically committed to a *post*-capitalist vision of global economic organisation. They want an amelioration of current conditions for the benefit of those who have been excluded or poorly served by economic globalisation. As will be apparent, this leaves a lot of possibilities open, so we need, firstly, to find some labels on which we can hang the myriad forms of reformist position. How to proceed?

'Strong' and 'weak' (liberal) reformisms

It is probably true to say that most people who have been present at anti-capitalist protests and marches are not anti-capitalist on a strict reading of the term – particularly the protests held in North America. They might be 'anti-globalisation', or 'anti-corporations', or they might not be anti-anything very large and abstract such as capitalism. However, it is true to say that anti-capitalist demonstrations are full of people who are opposed to what we have been calling *specific injustices*, such as a lack of rights for workers, or animals or indigenous peoples. They are also full of representatives of NGOs whose job it is to remedy specific injustices or to draw attention to discrete areas of policy making that require the attention of global elites, such as the condition of the environment, the supply of clean water or the need to abolish debt. To demonstrate against a specific injustice is to demonstrate against a *symptom* of global capitalism, something that is produced *by* global capitalism. Most of the time the call for the relief of such symptoms does not involve a threat or challenge to the global capitalist order itself, but rather a *limitation* on the capacity of capitalists to act in particular ways. Yet even the desire to limit capitalism is in some sense 'anti-capitalist' as capitalism is now constituted, that is as neoliberal capitalism. This is because (as we discussed in chapter 1) the thrust of neoliberalism is towards a *minimisation* of political constraints on the market. Neoliberals see limitations on the actions of capitalists as 'interfering with the market'. Anything that seeks either to re-impose limitations or to call for new ones is regarded as a threat to the self-regulating market order that underpins the 'Washington consensus'. Thus even modest forms of interventionism have been rendered anti-capitalist even where activists and lobbyists are reluctant to see themselves in such terms. The view that the task of the anti-capitalist or anti-globalisation movement is primarily to constrain or limit the actions of capitalists can, however, be more or less ideologically based. When it is ideological it resembles what might be termed *liberal internationalism*. When it is less ideologically driven it might be termed *liberal interventionism*. Let's start with the latter, which would on our typology represent the bottom right-hand corner, and then work our way up to more ideologically derived forms.

Liberal interventionism and the search for a 'compassionate globalisation'

Non or liberal interventionism equates to the view that, whilst the global order is far from perfect, the means of remedying many of the more significant injustices are already in place or are in the process of being brought into being. Reformers, which include the UN (particularly the UN Development Programme), many NGOs and elements of the global elite such as George Soros, Ted Turner and Bill Gates, start from the successful establishment of the post-1945 settlement, pointing to the manner in which institutions of global social and political governance have established an international order to which the vast majority of the world's nations have signed up. Others, including Barack Obama and the leaders of the EU, focus on the shared values they see as part of the post-war order, with its stress on the enlargement of the sphere of human rights and the necessity for responsible governance. For interventionists the problem is that such calls have all too often fallen on deaf ears when it comes to global corporations. This is to say that, whilst the discourse of human rights and common thresholds of decency as regards standards of living across the world have largely been accepted by policy-makers and forums such as the UN, corporations have been slow to respond in kind. Indeed, the record up to the present has been poor with environmental degradation, human rights abuses, sweatshop labour and child workforces all too often the price to be paid for keeping profit margins high. Thus the interventionist exhorts corporations to develop mission statements and charters professing their attachment to certain thresholds of decency and respect for workers and the environment. Clinton's emotive calls for a 'reformed' globalisation and Blair's similar call for 'compassionate' globalisation focused on the need for better links between labour and capital, for minimum rights for workers and limited debt relief. Clinton and Blair were not, of course, 'anti-globalisation'; but what they were calling for is in its own way similar to what many of those who do identify with such a position call for: a shift in the culture of global capitalism from a rapacious, anarchic free-for-all to an orderly and decent process that benefits the poor and needy rather than seeing them as so much fodder for profit maximisation.

As we noted in chapter 1, there is indeed a significant difference between the post-war order and earlier colonial and then imperial ages. Most nations can't do *exactly* what they want; similarly most companies can't do *exactly* what they want. To the interventionist, such observations are significant: nations and corporations have to obey – or be seen to obey – the legal and political framework set up after 1945 to regulate and limit the behaviour of national and supra-national actors. Not to do so would incur the prospect of being *shamed* into compliance by the insistence of international actors and global civil society that the culture as well as the letter of the rule of law be respected. Protesting is a process of shaming on this view. It is also a process of *lobbying* to have these powers extended and augmented by firmer controls, to have more laws where none exist, and to strengthen the capacity of the international order to regulate itself in accordance with them. Sometimes specific injustices are the result of the inadequacy of *existing legislation* and controls, and sometimes they are the result of inadequate or ineffective *implementation*. Liberal interventionism is the view that existing legislation has to be strengthened along with the machinery for its implementation. Thus liberal interventionist demands are typically issued in the form of rights. Workers need more rights – but so do turtles and indigenous peoples. This in turn presupposes a sovereign power able to enforce existing rights and propose new ones. Hence the central role that supra-national institutions play in liberal discourse generally. Nation-states and corporations cannot be trusted because they have interests they are zealous to protect.

Supra-national bodies like the UN, on the other hand, were set up to represent everyone's interests and thus can be charged with carrying out this internationalist and universalist function – so it is hoped.

Liberal interventionism therefore requires us to accept that:

- the particular and general interests of capital can be challenged by concerted pressure exercised from below, namely through protests, demonstrations, petitions and lobbying. Corporations can be made to feel guilty at betraying core or common values appearing in their mission statements and advertising. Capitalism can be made more caring and more responsible both to consumer and producer needs.

- the primary function of international institutions is to regulate international affairs in accordance with what is just and reasonable as opposed to what is in the interests of corporations or big business. The UN is not an arm of capital, but an independent court of appeal and lobbying organisation which, with some reforms, could be an effective weapon in the struggle against the abuse of the world's poor and weak.

- the position of the US as global 'hegemon' and as carrier of an ultimate veto against progressive measures is a potentially positive as well as negative factor in world affairs, offering the prospect that the US *could* underpin measures designed to benefit the whole – but only when led by enlightened *multilateralists* or left Democrats (like Clinton and Obama) – not narrow *unilateralists* or *neoliberals* such as Reagan, the Bushes and the leaders of the Tea Party.

- US politics is itself amenable to pressure from below to alter foreign as well as domestic policy in accordance with liberal principles as opposed to the interests of capital. The job of activists is to point continually to the discrepancy between what the US *says* it stands for and what it *does* or allows to take place in its name.

In their defence liberal interventionists can point to some significant successes. The extensive sweatshop campaigns organised across US campuses have signally embarrassed corporations such as Nike, Apple and Gap, and compelled them to take seriously the threat of boycotts and consumer strikes. As Klein documents in *No Logo*, such brands trade on their street credibility and sensitivity to the needs and aspirations of youth. Thus when youth is mobilised against them (as has occurred to an increasing degree in the US and elsewhere), they have to sit up and take notice. Campaigns such as these play capitalism's self-image against itself. They point to the contradictions inherent in the promise of the brand, thereby provoking – at least potentially – a consumer backlash and thus a threat to their profit margin. What they don't do is (according to critics) challenge the right of capitalism to hire labour or make huge profits out of the efforts of its reserve army labouring away in the tax-free, unregulated havens of the global South. Direct action of this kind also serves to highlight discrepancies between the values and ideals of the American political imaginary ('equality'; the 'Dream'; 'freedom') against the reality of misery and exploitation in sweatshops, in the export processing zones and *maquiladoras* of the developing world. As contemporary US history shows, progressive advances can be and are made on the basis of exploiting this gap between the promise and reality of US policy. Change might not occur as fast as radicals would like, and it might not go as far as critics demand. Nonetheless, without direct action of this kind the position of ethnic and racial minorities, of women, of the poor would in all probability be immeasurably worse than it is now.

We love the UN: liberal internationalism and the future of global governance

Although many activists particularly in the US would fall into the non-ideologically driven interventionist camp, there is a strong tradition both in the US and elsewhere, particularly Europe, of a more ideologically orientated form of reformism, the strains of which can occasionally be heard in the pronouncements of activists, NGOs, elites, academics and media figures. This is sometimes termed liberal or 'cosmopolitan' internationalism. The work of the philosopher Immanuel Kant who lived at the end of the eighteenth century remains the clearest statement of such a position, so it is worth briefly outlining his own much-utilised account of globalisation.

Kant considered himself a kind of realist in the sense that he regarded peoples and nations as characterised by what he termed 'unsocial sociability'. This is to say that he thought the primary dynamic of social life to be underpinned by our desire to realise our own 'ends', that is to secure our own wants and needs. These ends often clashed or contradicted the ends of others, necessitating rules and laws and thus institutions guaranteeing a certain freedom of movement and actions. Obeying these laws was regarded by Kant as the necessary price for social peace and our continuing capacity to act as autonomous or free individuals. Kant saw the problem of global peace as analogous to the problem of social peace. Different nations and cultures co-exist, each a limit to, as well as a means for, the realisation of the other's ends. This necessitates a system of international institutions that allow each nation or state to realise its own ends without having to submit to the threats or blandishments of the others. Such a conception was, we can add, very much at the forefront of the thinking of the founders of the UN. Relations between states had to be guided by laws which each would seek to live by, to the benefit of the whole. It is thus implicit to a Kantian approach that global institutions be strong enough to countermand the instructions and edicts of national institutions. It is also implicit that the relationship between global political institutions and economic institutions should weigh in favour of the former rather than the latter, and indeed that the latter should *themselves* come to be political, as opposed to narrowly economic in terms of character and function.

Kant's prognosis directly and indirectly underpins the position of those whose greatest concern is with the 'democratic deficit' we remarked on in chapter 1. As we noted there, global governance is currently characterised firstly by the predominance of economic considerations over political issues, which in turn reflects the neo-liberal belief in the priority of the market over the public sphere. To put the same matter differently, global politics is not really political at all in the sense that issues of global justice, of welfare and redistribution, are signally absent from the agendas of global institutions, and particularly those whose function has been expressed in narrowly economic terms, such as the IMF and World Bank. It is also characterised by the non-democratic nature of global institutions generally, making them amenable to the wishes of the most powerful capitalist states as well as to transnational capital. As becomes evident, one might regard such a position as 'anti-capitalist' in the sense that it is calling for the *re-politicisation* of the realm of the economy. Liberal internationalism calls for economic matters to become subject to political decision-making, which in turn directly contradicts the thrust of neoliberal orthodoxy. Assuming those political institutions were to become democratic then this would in turn open the way to a challenge to the rights of capitalists to organise their affairs with no care except for profit maximisation and accumulation. All these specific injustices would then have an outlet for their expression within the institutions themselves, allowing a full and continuous debate on the nature and course of global economic matters.

On the other hand, what is rarely suggested by those propounding such an approach is that capitalism itself should be overthrown or transformed. What is suggested rather is that neoliberal capitalism could be contested both regionally and at the global level by other models of capitalist development, in particular those permitting the setting of politically driven goals and objectives. This illustrates why such an approach has to be considered as *mildly* reformist. Internationalist approaches call for institutional reform and change, not for change and reform in the character of capitalist production itself. But we still need to be clear about what is on offer. What is institutional reform? How might this work?

Many reformists point to the non-democratic and unrepresentative nature of global institutions. Although the vast majority of states are represented on these bodies, their voices are heavily differentiated in favour of the major states of the North. Thus the UK, the US, France, China and Russia are all permanent members of the UN Security Council, whereas all other countries merely rotate, thereby ensuring that the interests of the major economic powers are paramount as regards issues of global security. At the IMF and the World Bank the distribution of votes and thus of influence and power follows the quota of funds that a given country makes available to them. Again, the result is that the voices of the US, the UK, France and other major states is dominant, which in turn means that corporate interests and the interests of the North come before those of the developing world. The G8, in which the eight wealthiest countries in the world come together to discuss matters of shared concern, is by definition a 'rich man's club' excluding the voices of poorer countries. Despite being based on the more egalitarian principle of 'one nation, one vote', the WTO's *rationale* is quite explicitly to promote free trade and open markets, thereby ruling out rival conceptions of global development. Most of its decisions are in any case the result of behind the scenes bargaining in the fabled 'Green Room' between countries of the wealthy North keen to maintain their privileged position in world trade. The result is that at the global level there is an implicit and sometimes explicit consensus in support of measures that favour the large corporations who in turn have a strong voice in determining the domestic agendas of political parties in the developed world.

Reform of the institutions thus focuses on two issues. The first is the *composition* of international bodies, and the second is their *role*.

In terms of *composition*, the argument advanced by institutional reformers is that if the developing world was given more of a say in the running of global institutions then it could be expected that they would develop policies that would favour their needs as opposed to the needs of corporate capitalism. Thus if the composition of the directorates of the World Bank and IMF were redrawn in favour of poorer nations then we could expect these institutions to develop policies in favour of the poorer countries. In particular we might expect them to be more lenient on the terms of debt repayment, or even to write off large chunks of debt accumulated over the past thirty years, as called for by prominent NGOs such as Jubilee 2000 and the World Development Movement. We might expect them to develop explicitly redistributionist policies encouraging developed countries to share with the developing world the patents and know-how that hold the latter back from developing. We might expect them to be more generous about the degree to which states are able to finance welfare programmes, schools and health-care. In particular we could expect a challenge to the neoliberal insistence on markets in favour of strategies for development that are mindful of the very differing priorities and needs of countries across the developing world. The insistence on a rigged variant of free trade in which the markets of the South are opened to the heavily state-subsidised goods of the North would, it could be expected, quickly be displaced by a variant of the fair trade policies many NGOs and politicians in the South see as a necessity. Fair trade would end the rigging of the market in favour of the North. It would prevent dumping, ensure that Northern producers rest within agreed norms of sustainable production and permit the unhampered flow of goods and services from South to North, in turn making possible the 'trickle-down' effect that liberal reformers see as essential to the moral case for capitalism.

Part of the assumption underpinning the demand for institutional reform is that the *role* of global bodies would change in perhaps radical ways. No longer would they be mere executors of the wishes of big business and the most powerful states; instead they would become arenas in which the diverse and plural needs of different states and regions could be aired and acted upon. As properly political bodies they would be open to diverse and plural conceptions of development, as opposed to development premised on the necessity for free markets, structural adjustment and cuts to public expenditure. The effect of such changes would be to narrow, if not cut completely, the democratic deficit that currently allows the interests of the rich and powerful to dictate to the rest of the world how and under what terms economic development is to take place. It would lead to what Walden Bello of the NGO Focus on the Global South terms 'deglobalisation', meaning the displacement of the free market by a conception of managed development in the interests of the global poor. Whether such reforms would in fact result in this kind of radical rebalancing of the global economy depends in turn on certain propositions about the nature of the global political scene and elite behaviour more generally. These could be summarised as follows:

- The most powerful countries would continue to support financially global institutions that are no longer under their direct or indirect control, or which have priorities other than those that are supportive of their own industries. Global institutions were created by the global rich to serve the interests of the global rich. For them to serve the interests of the global poor, a massive shift in the values and behaviour of Northern elites is required, the like of which would be quite unprecedented in global politics. Up to the present the US has been notoriously lax in paying its UN bills. How much laxer would US administrations become once power and influence shifted elsewhere – and particularly to the South?

- Transnational capital will not be able to blackmail reformed institutions into reintegrating their policies with the interests of transnational capital. Liberal internationalism puts its faith in the ability of institutions to exert influence over capital rather than vice versa (as many argue is the case now). This would require at the very least a transformation of US foreign policy away from the defence of national interests towards a policy of enlightened self-interest and a unilateral effort to cure the causes as well as the symptoms of global poverty.

- Political elites in developing countries are prepared to risk confronting transnational capital in the name of some non-free market model of economic development. One of the difficulties in the scenario envisaged here is that local and regional elites often ally themselves with the interests of capital, the US or both. This may be because they were put in power by the US or are maintained with the assistance of the US. Or it may reflect the willingness of local elites to enrich themselves through acceptance of the assistance offered by corporations. As post-war history illustrates, corruption of local elites is as much a *cause* of the South's miserable position as a symptom of it.

At the moment there has to be a question mark over all three assumptions about the prospects of institutional reform delivering substantive changes to the nature of economic globalisation. In particular it has to be questioned whether the US in its current mood would be inclined to go along with institutions that no longer reflect its interests, or the interests of US-based corporations.

'Strong(er)' reformism – or the return of social democracy

Milder variants of anti-capitalist reformism focus on institutions, trusting that, with a change in the nature of global institutions, substantive outcomes will improve particularly for poorer countries. As is evident, such an approach may have radical implications both in terms of the composition and the role of current global institutions. *May* have. There is enough uncertainty about the effect institutional reform would have to suggest to many that a more radical approach is needed, one that in effect guarantees certain *outcomes* as well as a certain reconfiguration of those institutions. It is one thing to argue that political institutions need to be reformed and quite another to argue that certain outcomes or a certain redistribution of wealth is just or more equitable. Institutional reform may produce radical outcomes, but of course it may not. Radical or strong reformisms are underpinned by the uncertainty of a narrowly institutional approach, preferring instead to present a more or less ideologically driven vision of how global wealth and opportunity should be configured. Again, the details vary between groups and activists, but what tends to inform this approach is the reinvigoration of what commentators term 'social democracy'.

Social democracy is a tradition of thought that dates back to the end of the nineteenth century. It is strongly associated with the organised labour movement and parliamentary labour parties that were created to defend the interests of working people. Today we hear social democratic demands being articulated by the International Confederation of Free Trade Unions (ICFTU), the Global Union Federations and the International Labour Organisation (ILO), as well as many well-known activists and intellectuals. What is perhaps novel about contemporary debates is that we find both those who favour a state-centred approach – aptly termed *national internationalism* – and others who favour a cosmopolitan approach with the object a *global state* with global powers of redistribution. But we need, firstly, to be clear about what, generally speaking, a social democratic approach amounts to.

Social democracy is a broad term that describes all those committed to making capitalism work for the interests of society generally, as opposed to the interests of big business and the well-off. Social democratic thought emerged initially as a critique of Karl Marx's demand for the overthrow of the capitalist order and the private ownership of the means of production. Early social democratic theorists such as Eduard Bernstein argued that capitalism was not doomed in the manner described by Marx and that class polarisation would not cause its downfall. Socialists and progressives thus had to adopt a more evolutionary approach to the task of developing a better society, using the productive energies unleashed by capitalist production to bring about more egalitarian policies. In this way they should nurture and promote capitalism's productive potential, whilst safeguarding the workers against the fluctuations of the trade cycle and flagging demand. Capitalism would be milked for the benefit of the thirsty masses, not just the capitalists themselves.

As social democratic thought developed in the early to mid-twentieth century, two considerations were uppermost in the thinking of social democrats in Europe. The first was the necessity for exercising *greater control over the market*, and the second was for *redistribution of resources* in accordance with some maxim of justice or equity. Control over the market was translated into 'demand-side economics', which is now associated with the work of the British economist John Maynard Keynes (hence 'Keynesianism'). It takes the view that the state has an *active* role to play in promoting capitalism and economic growth – as opposed to neoliberals who insist that only a passive or *laissez-faire* approach is appropriate. In particular the state should intervene to maintain demand, in turn the key to maintaining that economic growth and productivity without which, so it is held, modern societies would stagnate. Particularly in periods of economic down-swing, governments should borrow on the international money markets in order to invest in public works and public services, thereby providing the fuel for continuing demand and the basis for economic recovery, particularly in periods such as that following the GFC when money for private investment is hard to come by and thus where loss of jobs and stagflation are real threats. In its more radical form (i.e. as 'democratic socialism'), social democracy passes over into the belief in the necessity for socialistic measures to complement private economic activity, as for example in the demand for the nationalisation of major industries or 'the commanding heights of the economy'. The idea is that the state can manage the economic affairs of its constituency, eliminating or minimising the severe fluctuations which are otherwise part of the trade cycle as well as the mass unemployment and hardship that accompanies them. The state should steer the economy in ways that minimise the impact of recessions, whilst maximising the potential of the economy to return to full health and stability.

In terms of *redistribution*, an important part of the social democratic case is the belief that society will tolerate private ownership over the means of production if in turn it is palpably of benefit to ordinary citizens. Economic growth is not to be considered an end in itself, but rather a means to an end. This is the enrichment of society and the development of equality of opportunity, or more radically, (limited) equality of outcome. 'Equality of opportunity' is the belief that society should as much as possible eliminate factors preventing individuals from realising their full potential, such as poor housing, health or education. Equality of outcome additionally insists that the task of the state is to minimise – or even eliminate – the gap between the wealthiest and the poorest, thus necessitating very considerable state intervention. Social democracy thus enacts a kind of social *quid pro quo*. Business is able to get on with making money as long as in doing so it helps society and makes the lives of ordinary people, those who work for business, better. In turn business is furnished with a workforce that is better educated, healthier and less likely to regard continuing inequalities as a reason to resist the status quo. Social democracy was (and still is) unembarrassed about being a kind of 'capitalism with a human face', a way in which the worst excesses of capitalist exploitation could be offset by socially progressive measures that benefited everyone. Now its relevance lies in terms of promoting a vision of 'globalisation with a human face' – for the benefit of the vast majority and not just for the 'fat cats' of the global North. But how is such a transformation to be effected?

Social democracy as nationalist internationalism

It is on this point that social democratically inclined elements of the anti-capitalist movement diverge. The national international-ist position defends the view that the nation-state remains the pre-eminent actor in global affairs, and potentially the primary site of resistance to global capital. Irrespective of the desirability or otherwise of a global state, the development of such a state is, it is argued, a long way off. The nation-state is, however, still with us and can be mobilised to advance the cause of justice. Nationalist internationalists do not, however, argue for those old tools of national self-interest, protectionism and tariff barriers, to be re-erected (at least not in public). They argue that the best bulwark against untrammelled corporate power is for states to constrain the ability of transnational capitalists to move resources and production around the globe as they please. They point to the action taken, for example, by Malaysia to safeguard its economy in the wake of the 1997 Asian crisis. Refusing to stand mute before those scrabbling to shift their assets out of the country, Mohammed Mohathir imposed stiff penalties on the export of profits gained on the Kuala Lumpur stock exchange, a move which amazed many among the global elite for its sheer effron-tery, yet which also gained a measure of grudging respect from the IMF. Speculators took notice, with the effect that Malaysia was spared the worst effects of the crisis even though it was still very badly hit. If, so the argument goes, states acted together in terms of setting common policies on taxation, on the terms and conditions under which companies can set up, and on labour policies, then business would be less inclined to move around to seek optimum conditions and would thus be less able to destabilise the efforts of states to set macro-economic policies in the interests of their citizens. In other words, states should act *together* to increase the costs associated with moving production, thereby undermining the mobility and liquidity of capital. This would safeguard the jobs and social investment which are part of the social democratic deal for the citizens of individual nation-states. States need to bid each other *up* for the sake of keeping companies where they are, as opposed to bidding each other *down* (as they currently do) for the sake of attracting new capital as well as keeping companies already based in a given location.

The national state is moreover still the locus for social justice and for *redistribution* in accordance with nationally determined priorities. Again, national internationalists are sceptical about the degree to which such priorities could be determined at global level when there is evidently such enormous disparity in terms of wealth, culture, and infrastructure between North and South. No global state could overcome such disparities or make them disappear. Thus the right to higher education enjoyed by French students would be meaningless in a context where the population lacks elementary education and is functionally illiterate. What countries in the North can and must do, however, is shift resources to the South so that development and opportunity follow.

We still need to think, however, about the relationship of the national context to the international in 'nationalist internationalism'. What becomes apparent from the proposals is that the idea of the regional or continental bloc is an important part of the suggestion. Many leftists who support, for example, the idea of greater European integration do so on just such grounds, that is, because of the increased bargaining power the EU has vis-à-vis transnational capital as opposed to any given nation-state acting alone. As a bloc composed of nearly 400 million citizens, with four of the largest eight economies in the world on board, the EU can deploy considerable muscle in its relations with capital. In particular it could ensure that the near-constant outflow of productive capacity to central and eastern Europe as well as Asia and Latin America experienced over the past three decades is stemmed before it empties the EU completely of manufacturing. National internationalists argue that such moves cannot proceed on a unilateral basis. If they did then it would be little more than a form of Euro-nationalist protectionism. What is required rather is the development of analogous blocs elsewhere in the world. Thus they point to the potential of existing blocs such as Mercosur in Latin America or ASEAN in the Asia–Pacific region for providing a mutually supportive basis for such developments. If there were blocs of this kind covering all the world regions then the freedom to roam of transnational capital would be severely circumscribed. Corporations would no longer be able to seek out the cheapest labour, but would have to negotiate with regional administrations over conditions of entry into the relevant area. Speculative flows could be monitored and taxed, minimum labour standards set and public-private initiatives delivered for the benefit of local populations. In such fashion capitalism would be used to serve the varying needs and interests of local blocs, thus creating stability as well as a degree of equality as between different continents.

Again, we need to note that the credibility of such a position rests on certain key assumptions:

- There needs to be enough common interest within regional or continental blocs to maintain a united front in the face of corporate attempts to seek out low cost manufacturing environments. This is less a problem for the EU where moves to political as well as economic integration inch along, but more of a problem in the case of Asia, Africa or the Americas, where there is a great differentiation of wealth between countries. Poorer nations who may perceive the need for rapid inward investment in order to industrialise may be tempted to leave a bloc, perhaps temporarily, in order to increase inward investment vis-à-vis other members of the bloc.

- Similarly, at the global level there would have to be enough common interest to maintain a united front despite the massive inequalities between blocs and thus despite the considerable temptation low cost blocs may have to attract inward investment by whatever means possible. What is the incentive for, say, a South Asian bloc to act in solidarity with the European bloc so as to prevent the export of European jobs to India or Pakistan?

- The above in turn presupposes the availability of the political will as well as the ability to transfer massive resources from North to South in order to offset the effect of capital immobility and lack of investment. Presumably, Europeans and North Americans would be asked to subsidise the loss of inward investment experienced by less well-off blocs via some form of compensatory mechanism along the lines suggested by James Tobin, the Nobel Prize-winning economist, who suggested a tax on exchange rate transactions to dissuade speculation and provide funds for development projects. How long would such a policy remain popular with voters? How long before mutuality led to protectionism?

The suggestion admittedly involves some wishful thinking. Those blocs that currently exist, such as the EU and ASEAN, arguably perform in exactly the opposite way to that intended. As 'national leftists' and 'true internationalists' argue, the EU has so far imposed policies consonant with those of neoliberal orthodoxy, particularly as regards the necessity for balanced budgets, flexible labour markets, and reductions in social expenditure. Indeed the European Central Bank (ECB) has to date acted almost entirely in line with the strictures of the World Bank in imposing a deflationary regime orientated to generating economic growth at the cost of high levels of unemployment, a formula that could have been written by World Bank officials. The sovereign debt crisis of 2011–12 which saw the 'Troika' of the ECB, the EU and the IMF act in harness to discipline European states such as Greece, Ireland and Portugal reinforces the sense that the main purpose of international financial bodies is to safeguard the interests of banks and bondholders, if necessary through the imposition of austerity measures and the erosion of hard-won welfare and pension entitlements. Hardly the stuff of 'internationalism', however defined.

Looking at the global picture, prospects are hardly more encouraging. There seems little incentive for low-cost or highly productive economies to go along with a bloc-built consensus unless there is a massive compensatory mechanism to reassure them that they are not losing out. It would be interesting to hear the reactions of young people in Bulgaria, India or China, say, to the idea that what they need is *less* inward investment rather than more. How much compensation would have to be paid to convince people who have been raised on a diet of trickle-down economics, that there will be no trickle-down after all – but only some sort of recompense for lost opportunity? As NGOs like Forum for the Global South fear, national internationalism may become just a supra-national nationalism. This is particularly so where its advocates fail to show how a block on the movement of productive resources will aid those who currently look forward to the in-flow of resources caused by capital flight, the very phenomenon that encourages the wealthy to look to protectionist measures to defend their own workforce.

'We are the world': towards global justice

Arguably the most radical and certainly the most idealistic variant of reformism is that associated with the demand for a world government that would promote some form of global justice. If not an explicit demand of many NGOs campaigning on issues to do with development, third world debt, environmental degradation and poverty, the demand for global or cosmopolitan justice is part of the background noise of many of their policy documents and public announcements. This approach is associated with many prominent academics and commentators on globalisation including David Held, Richard Falk and George Monbiot, a prominent British commentator and campaigner. It is also intrinsic to the approach of many left liberals who argue for a radicalisation of the terms of the debate about the obligations of those in the global North vis-à-vis the global South. Notable advocates of global justice on these terms include Thomas Pogge, Amartya Sen, Philippe van Parijs and Martha Nussbaum. To advocates such as these the nation-state has already been surpassed as a locus for considering matters of equality and justice, which are now fully transnational or global in scope. What is required is concerted action at the *global* level, not merely to provide an institutional bulwark against the worst effects of capitalist globalisation, but an *alternative* model of economic and social justice, one that guarantees a certain minimum of security, well-being and environmental protection for all, not just to those who luckily find themselves in an effective or wealthy bloc. There are, it needs to be noted, many variants on the theme of global justice, but most of them share certain core ideas or concerns. These might be summarised in terms of the need to establish the *global management of economic affairs*; to enhance and augment *security*; to promote *justice and well-being*; to develop mechanisms of *accountability, representation and participation*; to foster the notion of *global citizenship*. Let's look briefly at the more significant elements.

In terms of economic affairs, cosmopolitans such as these look forward to the displacement of the free market by what might be termed a constrained market, that is a market in which capital is required to observe and obey certain basic principles, such as health and safety provision, pension and health-care requirements, and holiday entitlements. More radical suggestions tend to emphasise the necessity for agreed universal minimum standards and rates of pay for every worker. Less radical demands emphasise the necessity to tailor provision in accordance with local labour conditions, and prevailing rates of pay. In other words, less radical versions see the continuation of regional and local markets as inevitable, if not desirable. However, most global social democrats agree that people should have access to certain minimum standards in terms of housing, sanitation, supply of clean water, and education. At the macro-economic level the suggestion is that public management would offset the worst effects of capitalist globalisation in terms of the massive in-flow and out-flow of assets and resources, as per the Asian economic crisis of 1997/8, and the European sovereign debt crisis of 2011–12. Just as states currently work in partnership with companies to underwrite the costs and risks associated with development, so a global state would negotiate with corporations to ensure that the latter are not over-exposed in terms of the risks involved in setting up in the developing world. They envisage various forms of partnership with transnational capital to ensure a proper trade-off between risks and rewards for both business and the concerned workforce. What is uppermost is the desire to get away from the exploitative and demeaning sweat-shop conditions that much of the world's population currently endures.

Some globalisers further imagine a kind of global planning with decisions on economic management made in the sub-committees of a global parliament. As with national social democracy there is considerable variation in the degree to which activists and commentators see the management of macro-economic policy taking place. Some urge the Scandinavian model of high corporate tax as the way to shackle business to the political agenda of a global government. Others see a French-style *dirigisme* with a significant planning element and control or even nationalisation of important or key industries as the only way to guarantee that companies would be made to obey their political masters. And of course there are many other models of managed capitalism, from the Rhineland model of responsible corporatism, to the British or Gaitskellite (after the Labour politician) emphasis on increasing economic growth in the name of greater equality.

As regards *social justice*, a global state would assure everyone a certain minimum standard of living. This would be through some form of global taxation system in which the global rich subsidise the global poor. This could be achieved either through taxation on global flows or through direct taxation of individual and corporate earnings. Nevertheless, the key point is to get the wealthy to pay for the development of the South. This would already be an advance on the status quo in which individuals and corporations may legally use off-shore havens and zero-tax areas to hide their wealth from the governments of nation-states. As globalisers point out, huge amounts of income are currently off-limits to governments, necessitating at least *some* form of global intervention to bring the wealthy to account. Instead of confronting capital with a begging bowl, NGOs hope to appeal to the self-interest of Northern economies which look to expand consumption and thus boost production. Such a plan would be administered by global actors, perhaps foreshadowing greater partnership between the now burgeoning global civil society and mechanisms of global governance. In any case, as many NGOs argue, without such mechanisms poor countries will sink further into the vicious circle of under-development, poverty and instability. Global governance on this reading is not some form of luxury, another layer of bureaucracy to be paid for by the hard-pressed taxpayers of the North. It is the only way in which massive and growing inequalities can be addressed in effective and immediate ways.

The same is true for *anti-monopoly mechanisms*, that is, mechanisms which prevent corporations establishing themselves as sole suppliers for goods and services and thus exploiting their position for immense gains, usually at the cost of the impoverished consumer of the developing world. Campaigns against genetically modified goods and against the deployment of patents to generate immense profits for pharmaceutical companies trading on the HIV/AIDS epidemic in Africa stem from such concerns. Again, they point to the need to beef up global regulation of corporations to bring an end to the exploitation of those who are ill-equipped to fight back.

This in turn highlights the necessity for global institutions to promote *security and democratic governance* against the onslaught of predatory globalisation. In terms of security, an unfettered free market is regarded as the economic analogue of a political free-for-all or state of nature in which the strongest usually win, often at the cost of the common good. Pollution and environmental degradation are persistent themes, with globalists maintaining that without properly constituted global protocols – and the means of implementing them – the rich can always opt out of agreements to suit their own selfish needs, usually to the detriment of the less well-off. But, as recent history shows, sometimes countries in the developing world are their own worst enemies, and they need to be encouraged to work within stable and universally agreed norms in order not to degrade their own environments in the haste to meet their own population's ever-expanding needs. Only a global regulatory framework would be able to make both rich and poor sign up to green policies, safeguarding the interests of the global commons, and defending the interests of future generations who are of course unable to defend their need for sustainable production, a clean and stable climate and an educated, enabled workforce.

Security concerns often have a wider orbit as well in such demands, encompassing the need for strengthened control on arms proliferation which again is often sponsored or underwritten by wealthy nations of the North keen to sell the latest weapons and gadgets to governments in the developing world which are worried about threats from neighbours, themselves armed by western companies. A system of *global conflict management* would, so it is argued, help reduce regional and local rivalries, thereby diminishing the fear of armed force and permitting an open dialogue between countries that have sometimes been goaded on by wealthier onlookers seeking to support their arms industries. A system based on nation-states is one likely to maintain insecurity and the need for armaments. A system of global governance and universal mediation is likely to reduce global tensions and would promote much needed expenditure on welfare and social security. Similarly, global governance would, it is anticipated, institutionalise a global dialogue of the kind that has been singularly lacking throughout the history of the modern world, yet which is needed to underpin the rights of minorities and cultural diversity. Without such a system, diversity is regarded as a threat, a 'clash of civilisations' between apparently irreconcilable cultures. Here is an echo of the Kantian theme touched on above of the desirability and indeed necessity for humanity to reconcile itself to co-existence and co-operation. Without it, so the argument goes, the globe will forever remain hostage to those with economic, as well as perhaps cultural and religious, reasons for promoting antagonism and conflict. To cosmopolitans the best means of avoiding such an outcome is the institutionalisation of dialogue and the elaboration of rights that protect cultural differences, however constituted.

Finally, reformists stress the need for the democratisation of global institutions and the development of an ethic and practice of *global citizenship*. The issue of the democratic deficit looms large once again, with many critics and activists voicing their concern about the lack of accountability, representation and opportunities to participate at the global level. The existence of a global civil society, of different groups, NGOs, and other non-state actors is testament, so it is claimed, to the existence of a global constituency and thus of the need for institutions and procedures in which the constituency can be heard. Here, however, opinion again divides. Milder variants tend to focus on the immediate need for the formalisation of representation for NGOs and particular interests in existing institutions, such as the UN and the WTO. This is to say that global civil society (i.e. NGOs) should be listened to or, better, represented in existing structures of decision-making. More robust variants stress the necessity for wholesale changes to the system of governance, permitting the development of a global state proper perhaps through an extension of the UN, with directly or indirectly elected parliamentary chambers and global elections for global parties. This would be a globalisation of the form of representative democracy we find in social democratic states with perhaps increased safeguards for the rights of minorities, mechanisms for rendering both private and public actors accountable, funding for global lobbyists and access to the global media. There are many variants on the theme, reflecting the many variants of representative democracy available around the globe. However, certain themes tend to stand out in such schemes, for example:

- the necessity for *multi-level governance*, meaning systems in which decisions can be taken at the appropriate level (subnational, national, regional, continental, global) or in consultation with the appropriate constituency (developing countries, agricultural regions, areas experiencing famine, religious minorities). Few in other words argue for a unitary or UK-style state with a powerful centralised authority, but rather a heavily tiered representative system fully embracing 'subsidiarity' – the principle that decision-making is made by representatives at the level nearest to those affected by the outcome.
- the need for *transparency and accountability*. Those who govern should be subject to rigorous checks from below whether by

parliamentary committee, the media or other constituents. This would be in contrast with the secretive or heavily veiled meetings of global institutions like the IMF and the WTO where most of the business is conducted in the 'green room', i.e. in private.

• the need for *sensitivity to cultural diversity, tradition, and the rights of minority groups and peoples*. A necessary feature of any progressive equivalent of global structures would be to make them responsive to the very different needs and values of the world's populations. This points to constitutional safeguards for religious practices, minority media outlets, multilingual structures.

In short the narrow concern 'with who gets what, how and when?' needs to be augmented by the contemporary liberal concern to ensure parity of treatment, a secure or constitutionally based system of human rights and group rights. It also needs to be complemented with the green concern to provide a basis for sustainable development or patterns of economic activity that are less damaging than the more or less unfettered market system we have at present. Citizenship must in this sense not only be genuinely global, but genuinely inclusive of those who might otherwise be excluded. In short, social democracy would have to be genuinely universalist whilst paying great attention to the needs and interests of the very many minorities, groups, nations and peoples that compose the globe.

Could global reform work – for whom?

Defenders of approaches such as these consider themselves realists in the sense that often their arguments are framed with a view to countering or challenging those further to the left than themselves. It is probably true to say that on these terms it is indeed more realistic, if only in the sense that it asks quite a lot less of elites than do Marxists or other revolutionary groups. It proposes to *ask* global elites to give up some of their power and privilege rather than to *divest* them of it, as is implied in radical approaches. Nonetheless, viewed from the perspective of the present, 'global justice' looks uncompromisingly radical from the point of view of the wild frontier of global capitalism. This is particularly so viewed from the position of the US, which virtually alone among the advanced capitalist countries has little in the way of a social democratic or left liberal tradition to draw on to make the comparison. This is a particularly important point in that it is noticeable that the argument for global justice tends to work by *analogy*. What this means is that those who advocate global justice rely on transferring arguments that have been seen as compelling at the national level to the global level. To take an example from contemporary Britain, we frequently hear the complaint that health-care is better in some important respect in one part of the country immediately followed by the demand that the situation be remedied. Don't we all pay our taxes? Don't we all in this sense have a right to the same level of health-care? What we rarely hear by way of a reply is that people in one part of Britain pay proportionately far more in taxes than do those in some other poorer part, and so should have access to better health-care. In this sense health issues in the UK are still dominated by a social democratic discourse that insists on equality of access and equality of services *irrespective* of the ratio of payment either individually or at local or regional level. Citizenship in such a context implies equality of access to resources provided by the state no matter where one finds oneself.

What cosmopolitans hope is that just as most people in the UK do not query British people's right to equal health-care, so they will not query the right of people across the world to, if not equal health-care, then let's say some *adequate* health-care (relative to some internationally agreed norm). What they hope is that just as we accept certain obligations towards our fellow citizens here, so we will accept certain obligations to everyone. We will come (or are coming) to see the population of the world as in some way analogous to the way citizens in social democratic countries view their fellow citizens: not just as consumers or workers or capitalists, but as people with particular needs that it is our duty to help satisfy. This is what it means to live in a civilised society; this is what it *should* mean to live in a civilised world.

It is a noble sentiment, but one that many would argue is actually in relative decline where it once existed, and a far-off communitarian ideal in countries where it never existed. As writers such as Robert Putnam and Zygmunt Bauman lament, the tendency of modernisation is towards greater *individualisation* rather than the generation of greater community spirit. If such commentators are to be believed, we as modern citizens increasingly lack 'social capital'. We lack that stock of associations and bonds that takes us out of our otherwise solitary existences and places us in a social context where we can see how important we are to others and in turn how important others are for the realisation of our goals and aspirations. Thus according to the relevant data we increasingly resent the community or social obligations we are said to owe to others. We don't like paying taxes, particularly when those taxes are used to fund services for particular groups, causes or minorities with whom we ourselves feel little sympathy. For philosophers such as David Miller the ideal of global justice advanced by cosmopolitan thinkers is a delusion. Experience tells us that the nation is probably the largest aggregate body to which most of us feel any attachment or affinity. Justice is therefore justice for those who live within the *nation-state*. It can never be universal or global.

So much for the bleak prognostications of academic research. It is probably true that the effort to generate genuinely global sentiments represents an idealistic gesture of Herculean proportions.

But what cosmopolitans can point to is that if globalisation has had one effect in the cultural domain then it is in terms of the increased awareness of our proximity to others. The term 'global village' is an awful cliché; but it is one that nonetheless speaks to an important aspect of contemporary consciousness. People are getting 'nearer' to each other, nearer in terms of the time it takes to communicate with others across the globe, nearer in terms of time to get *to* other parts of the world, nearer in terms of the lag between events occurring and their appearing on our TV screens. But we are also forced to be near in terms of global political problems: environmental degradation, climate change, international conflict, poverty caused by international trade agreements, the GFC. 'Nearness' (or 'proximity') must be a key factor in thinking about who is relevant to our lives, to whom we feel a duty of care, with whom we feel some sense of solidarity. Our obligations are therefore universal rather than regional, national or local.

Before leaving the subject it is however important to consider the politics of these positions. As we mentioned above, left liberals and social democrats have historically regarded themselves as realists, particularly when set alongside those we shall shortly consider. Yet the grounds of social democratic realism were much more apparent than now in the case of the welfare states they helped develop a century ago. Social democracy prospered because it was able to take advantage of the development of universal suffrage across Europe in the nineteenth and early twentieth century. By appealing to the interests of the newly enfranchised, social democrats were able to utilise the collective power of the masses to further policies of social justice and demand management. The difficulty with transferring the social democratic analogy across to the contemporary situation is that there is no global state to speak of, nor much of a prospect of one being created given the powerful forces lined up to ensure that such a state remains a pipe dream. This underlines the degree to which the call for global justice is on almost any definition a radical – even utopian – one rather than a realistic one under contemporary conditions. Indeed, advocates of global justice find themselves in the position of the Jacobins rather than the Victorian progressives they sometimes sound like. Like the former they need to create political authority first, and *then* attempt to deploy it for whatever egalitarian and redistributive measures it is agreed should be pursued. Whether this can be done politely, that is, without holding a gun to the heads of global elites – for example through the threat of withholding debt repayments as advocated by Monbiot – is a matter of intense debate both within and without reformist circles.

4

A 'movement of movements' II: renegades, radicals and revolutionaries

In the last chapter we considered the anti-capitalism of the reformers: an anti-capitalism that is anti-corporate power, anti-neoliberal or anti-the-free-market, but not anti-capitalist on a strict reading of the term. They do not call for an end to the private ownership of the means of production, to wage labour or to production for profit, as opposed to some other principle. This is not to say that reformist anti-capitalisms are not themselves radical. As we discussed, under current conditions most schemas that stray from acceptance of the market and passive acceptance of the neoliberal agendas of global institutions have an undeniably radical air to them. Nevertheless, they call for a modification of global capitalism, not its elimination or transformation. In Part Two of our analysis we look at those who *are* in some fundamental respect anti-capitalist on these terms. In particular we need to cover the three main radical groupings: *Marxist and neo-Marxist* groupings, *anarchism* and radical *environmentalism*. By way of a contrast to these more or less ideologically driven positions we also look at *Zapatismo*, the ideas and analysis of the Zapatistas and their spokesperson Subcomandante Marcos.

Marxism after the 'fall of communism'

It may come as a surprise after all we have said about the death of Marxism or communism in chapter 2 to begin a consideration of the radical wing of anti-capitalism with Marxist groups. If Marxism is 'dead', then why are we looking at it? Attentive readers of the relevant chapter will have noted that one of the key distinctions drawn in the exposition was between 'official' and 'unofficial' politics, that is between national politics, the politics of electioneering, political parties and voting, and the subterranean unofficial politics that began to proliferate after 1968. What we noted there was that official Marxism – the Marxism of the Communist Bloc – went into decline after that point and eventually succumbed in all but a handful of countries after the Fall of the Berlin Wall in 1989. China, the most powerful of the remaining communist regimes, appears increasingly embarrassed about its Marxist-Leninist heritage, and rightly so given its enthusiasm for capitalism. On the other hand, unofficial Marxism – the Marxism that vehemently *criticised* the Soviet Union, the Communist Bloc as well as the West – has never gone away. Indeed as is evident, Marxist groups have been amongst the most important and most visible at anti-capitalist protests, particularly in Europe. Marxist writers such as Alex Callinicos, Slavoj Žižek, David Harvey and John Holloway have offered compelling analyses of contemporary society as well as prescribing programmes and strategies for an anti-capitalist resistance. Many Marxist groups are well-organised and well-furnished with the means of making their presence felt, whether it be in the preparation of banners and placards, in the printing of posters, leaflets and newspapers, or in organising carnivals, festivals, summer schools and teach-ins. Marxists have been prominent in organising anti-capitalist protests and initiatives.

To suggest, however, that the relative success of Marxist groups in attaining prominence is due to superior organisation and resources is to ignore the central fact about Marxism. This is that the works of Marx offer the oldest, most sophisticated and most complete account of capitalism and its travails. Marxism offers a critique of capitalism in all its dimensions, ethical, moral, political and economic. It also offers a ready account of what it is that should replace capitalism, and offers some indications of how to get there. None of which is to say that what Marx wrote has to be regarded as compelling, convincing or indeed correct in some relative or absolute sense. As we shall see, there are many radicals within the anti-capitalist movement who argue that not only was Marx wrong in some important sense, but also that Marxism is a pernicious and harmful doctrine that has to be isolated and combated wherever possible. Nonetheless it is also a truism to note that Marxism is *one* of the most, if not *the* most, important currents of anti-capitalist thought and practice and merits consideration on these terms alone. Getting clear about what Marxism offers will also help us to get clear about the two other principal radicalisms of the anti-capitalist movement, anarchism and environmentalism, as well as the many hybrid positions between them.

Anyone who has been on an anti-capitalist demonstration or who has followed the fortunes of radical politics will know that that there are literally hundreds of Marxist groups or groupuscles around the world. Their names generally contain at least two of the following terms: 'Marxist' (and/or-'Leninist'), 'socialist'/ 'communist','people's'/'workers','party'/'movement'/'tendency', 'international', 'revolutionary' and 'popular'. Sometimes the name of the relevant host country is appended, helpfully making clear the point of origin of the particular group in question. Some of these groups are tiny, no more than a handful of hardy souls producing a newsletter or leaflet. Others are much larger. According to a 2008 BBC report, the UK Socialist Workers Party (SWP) is said to have around 7,000 members. There are significant Marxist groupings in Italy, France and Spain. Marxism remains an important current in Greek and Turkish politics, in the politics of many Asian countries such as India, and also in Latin America and South Africa. Indeed, the only places with little or no Marxist activity is in former Communist regimes, where unsurprisingly anything associated with the old order is often looked upon with disdain. Nonetheless the appeal of Marxism to *activists* is significant, and it is easy to see why.

Firstly, Marxism offers an intellectually coherent and highly sophisticated analysis of capitalism, one that like all great doctrines stems from an essentially simple idea. This is that capitalist production represents a form of exploitation. Capitalism is initiated through the appropriation of the basic resources that we require to live an independent existence, particularly the land taken over in the global process of 'primitive capitalist accumulation'. Having dispossessed people of the land, capitalists then exploit those without the means of their own subsistence, paying them a fraction of the value they produce and keeping the rest as profits. Yet the critique of capitalism is not *merely* moral or ethical in nature, as it is for certain strands of anarchism and socialism, but one based on the certainty that capitalism is unsustainable over the long term. It is also based on a particular conception of rationality and human progress that insists on the *necessity* for capitalism as a prelude to the construction of 'higher' forms of social life. This illustrates an important fact about Marx's work, which is that he believed that without modernisation, industrialisation and the wholesale transformation of life that goes along with it, there could be no socialism, let alone communism. Marx was in this sense a creature of the Enlightenment. Whilst he was deeply pained by the spectacle of capitalist production, he was a great admirer of the advances made under capitalism in the field of production. What angered him was that production was for profit rather than the satisfaction of human needs. Private property was a right enjoyed by the few, not the many. Capitalism had in this sense prepared the way for a higher form of existence, but was itself the obstacle to its realisation. It thus had to be overthrown by the class that capitalism itself creates, namely the 'proletariat' or working class.

Even on the basis of this minimal description we can glean certain important facts about Marxist approaches to resistance and the nature of the post-capitalist order to come. Firstly, Marx looked to the working class to be the agent of change. At one level this was simply because he thought that the tendency of capitalist production was to reduce the number of classes to two, namely the proletariat and the bourgeoisie. But on another it was because he thought that what made people potentially revolutionary was the *experience* of being exploited or alienated. Intellectuals like himself could empathise with labour, but historically they were just as likely, if not more so, to side with the owners. For workers, who actually experienced increased competition and exploitation, there was little choice. It was fight back or succumb to a life of servitude and squalor. Marx also saw that advanced production, particularly factory production, made for a different kind of individual, one used to working *collectively*. Working together gave people the impetus to *act* together against a common enemy and in common cause. These and other factors made him invest his hopes and expectations in the proletariat.

Secondly, it is important to note that Marx was a communist, not a socialist. He considered socialism a stage *on the way to* communism. This is to say that he looked forward to the *complete* abolition of private property, of classes, of fundamental distinctions between peoples, nations, individuals. He also looked forward to the complete abolition of the state, the police, the judicial apparatus and everything else that went with it. If this sounds like Marx was an anarchist, then we should point out that the First International, created in 1864 included anarchists as well as communists and socialists, the distinctions then being perhaps less sharp than they are now. Marx *was* a kind of anarchist. Indeed he often accused his anarchist opponents such as Pierre-Joseph

Proudhon and Mikhail Bakunin of not being consistent enough in their opposition to the state. But his 'anarchism' involved, paradoxically, a great deal of organisation, too much for his anarchist critics. This is a reasonable point. Marx wanted a highly advanced, highly industrialised form of life, one that surrendered nothing in its progress towards a better world; but he *also* wanted individuals to be fully involved in all the decisions affecting them. He thought planning offered the best means of ordering an economy (as he made clear in *The Communist Manifesto*); but he also looked forward to the *complete* decentralisation of decision-making as described in his sympathetic portrayal of the Paris Commune of 1871. He wanted the individual to develop all her potential, to become 'many-sided', but he *also* wanted her to feel at one with the collective. He wanted the proletariat to emancipate itself, but he also wrote in terms of the necessity for the Communist Party to show the proletariat 'the line of march', thereby implying that it could not emancipate itself without the help of intellectuals and the 'most advanced' sections of the class organised above and beyond the 'less' advanced.

The (many) sons and daughters of Marx

The above points give us a clue as to why there are so many competing Marxisms on offer, with so many different groups and parties all jostling for our attention. Some groups emphasise the need for planning, others the needs for local or decentralised decision-making. Some stress the necessity for the party or movement to lead; others stress the capacity of ordinary people for self-organisation. Some stress Marx's attachment to a strict historical timetable, inferring that revolution can only be legitimate at a certain point of historical development; others stress the contingent or self-determining nature of the historical process, implying that revolution will occur whenever ordinary people, as opposed to economic indicators, say it is ready. Some think that all these different aspects of Marx's approach can be integrated into a non-contradictory and perfectly consistent whole. The point is, none of these interpretations is wrong, because all of them can be found in some corner or other of Marx's vast opus. And if they cannot be found there, then they can be found in one of Marx's authoritative followers such as Lenin or Trotsky, or Gramsci or whomever.

This in turn illustrates what is particularly distinct about Marxism as a politics: it relies very heavily on *the use and interpretation of texts*, not just those of Marx, but also of Marx's followers. Marxist groupings seek to develop a 'line' on all the key issues of the day, and this is informed by a continual reading and rereading of works by Marx and his followers. In this sense asking why there are so many Marxisms is akin to asking why there are so many different Christian churches and sects. Where doctrines rely on the interpretation of texts one is almost bound to have schism, particularly where there are *so many* texts. There is only one Bible (or two Testaments), but the *Collected Works of Marx and Engels* (aptly shortened to the 'MEGA') run to fifty volumes at the last count. The further point is that whilst Marx *was* a remarkably consistent thinker, he was also a remarkably adaptable one, or, to put it less charitably, he could say something on one occasion and appear to contradict himself on another. This is fun for scholars of Marx to pick over, but politically it means that there is a continual sparring between and amongst Marxists on certain crucial issues, like the role of the party, or the nature of the 'transition' between capitalism and communism, the exact moment when revolution becomes legitimate. As a result there is not one Marx, but lots of Marxs, and we can add lots of Lenins and Trotskys too.

But isn't there something, some essential core to Marxism that will help the beginner decide if and to what degree it holds anything of any use to him or her? Here we need to be brave and suggest the following as a rough guide to what Marxism means as a variety of anti-capitalism:

- *the primacy of productive processes and thus of class struggle for 'reading' anti-capitalism*. Other kinds of struggle, for example, for human rights or environmental measures, are all in some sense secondary and thus subordinate to economic considerations 'in the final analysis'. They are symptoms of capitalist oppression, and thus can only be alleviated by overthrowing capitalism itself. This in turn helps explain why Marxists get accused of cynicism in their relations with groups who see Marxists as reducing all oppressions to one: that of the working class.

- *the necessity of working class organisation for defeating capitalism*. Only the working class, acting *as a class*, has the power to defeat capitalism. This is because it is only the withdrawal of labour that really damages the capitalist class, particularly as, on a Marxist reading, it is labour that creates value for the capitalist. From this point of view Marxists utterly reject the view described in chapter 2 that the working class is dead or irrelevant to an anti-capitalist movement.

- *necessity for a party or movement to oversee the revolutionary process and initiate measures needed to begin the transition to communism*. To be successful a revolutionary assault on capitalism requires organisation, planning, strategy, tactics. All this in turn implies the necessity for self-organisation via a party or movement with a leadership which is able to prosecute its aims and objectives.

- *transfer of the means of production into the hands of the workers* (or those representing their interests). Ultimately anti-capitalism is about the reappropriation of the productive resources of the world for humanity as a whole. This may involve bloodshed, but in Marx's view need not necessarily do so. Indeed, he was happy in his own writings to tinker with more or less gradual ways in which to transfer the productive wealth of the few into the hands of society through nationalisation, joint stock companies and the like.

- *socialism is a transitionary stage on the way to communism.* Socialism can never be considered an end in itself. Communism is the *complete* abolition of private property and the market. Under communism distribution of goods would be in accordance with 'needs', not 'work', let alone any market-derived formula. Marx was an avowed *critic* of socialist and social democratic notions of egalitarianism and distributive justice.

Compared with the positions we have described so far this is a radicalism of a spectacularly uncompromising kind. It foretells the collapse of capitalism, the elimination of all fundamental differences between nations, peoples and religions and the creation of a 'society of associated production' on a global scale. It is precisely the radicalism that attracts Slavoj Žižek, perhaps the best-known Marxist, indeed Leninist, theorist of the moment. A thinker who combines a deep knowledge of continental thought, psychoanalytic insights drawn from the work of Jacques Lacan, and a wonderful eye for the paradoxes of pop culture, Žižek revels precisely in the qualities that make others so suspicious of Marxism as a political practice. In his view one of the reasons why Fukuyama was able to declare the 'end of history' was that the left had given up contesting the legitimacy of capitalism. It had retreated to a safe 'postmodern' style of analysis, obsessed with cultural differences and identity politics. It had convinced itself that capitalism was 'natural' as a prelude to convincing others that they had to concentrate on narcissistic lifestyle, self-improvement, multicultural politics and safe, inclusive forms of political discourse and practice. All of this promoted a '*Denkverbot*' or veto against naming the enemy: capitalism. The GFC of course changed all this, much to Žižek's delight. The problem, however, remains in convincing those raised on a diet of postmodern theorising that only a robust politics aimed at overthrowing capitalism and bringing about a communist order in which society regains control over its own productive capacities can save us from what he terms 'the end of times'. In short, we need to rediscover a militant Leninist style of politics, however unfashionable or unreasonable it may seem to some.

After Leninism: autonomism, council communism, and 'heterodox' radicalism

Notwithstanding the above discussion, it needs to be asserted that Marxism can be more or less ideological as we are using the term here. This is to say that there are Marxists who are stubbornly doctrinal in their approach, holding that there is only one correct version of Marx's work, only one correct vision of anti-capitalist politics, and only one correct view of what a post-capitalist society could be like. Sectarianism is and always has been endemic in Marxist circles for precisely this reason.

Yet there are also Marxists (and revolutionary socialists) who are much less committed to maintaining a doctrinal or ideological line in this sense and thus are more willing to regard the process of revolutionary struggle as one involving working class *self*-organisation and *self*-understanding. Chief amongst these would be the various 'autonomist' or non-Leninist Marxisms. Some of these date back to the earliest years of the Russian Revolution and the failure of the Bolsheviks to deliver the Soviet democracy promised by Lenin on coming to power. In this sense autonomist Marxism was a direct challenge to Bolshevism and to the idea of the Soviet Union as the locus for anti-capitalist initiatives. Early council communists such as Anton Pannekoek, Paul Mattick and Karl Korsch focused on the possibilities inherent in the soviets or workers' councils as a basis for social organisation. They stressed the need for decentralisation of decision-making, a high degree of communal or cantonal autonomy and the need for vigilance against the encroachments of the state and large-scale bureaucracy of the sort developing in the Soviet Union. Autonomist Marxism received a major boost in 1968, particularly in France where the Situationist critique, looked at briefly in chapter 2, accelerated the rejection of traditional party structures by many leftists.

As regards developments post-1968, the currency of autonomist ideas and themes is pervasive, particularly in Italy which, with Germany and Holland, has a strong autonomist tradition in thought and action. All three have significant networks of autonomists in major cities with extensive activities, support groups, established facilities for squatters, lobby groups, and micro-economic structures. In terms of distinct groupings high profile autonomist networks include *Ya Basta!* (Enough!) formed after 1994 in solidarity with the Zapatista rebellion. Along with the *Tuti Bianchi* and the WOMBLES (or 'White Overalls Movement Building Libertarian Effective Struggles'), they have been a colourful presence at the larger anti-capitalist demonstrations. Elsewhere there are a huge number of autonomist collectives, groupuscles and affinity groups, including those associated with journals and newsletters such as *Fifth Estate*, *Aufhebung* and *Midnight Notes*. Some of the more interesting analyses of the contemporary picture are written by those of an autonomist bent such as Michael Hardt and Toni Negri, whose trilogy, *Empire*, *Multitude* and *Commonwealth* is a much read – and much puzzled over – contribution to the genre. We should also mention the work of John Holloway whose *Change the World Without Taking Power* and *Crack Capitalism* are widely read in activist as well as academic circles.

Given this diversity of autonomist perspectives it would stretch matters to talk about an autonomist movement as such. Indeed as is will be evident looking at their publications and websites, there is as much bickering about correct interpretations of key thinkers and theories amongst autonomist factions as there is within Marxism. Nonetheless it is evident that autonomism is a key current of contemporary anti-capitalist resistance and so needs to be thought about further. So how could we summarise what it stands for as a tradition of thought and action?

- Autonomism and its various currents such as 'Operaismo' stress the open nature of the historical process and thus the *importance of political struggle over economic forces*. Indeed certain variants of autonomism would assert that economic forces are themselves determined by class struggles, thereby reversing the line developed by many of Marx's orthodox followers. The significance of such a move theoretically is that it leads to a more militant style of politics, one that accentuates the impact that radical and trade union activism can have on the ability of capitalism to maintain itself. 'Crisis' is read here less as an objective feature of the capitalist system, than a function of working class militancy.

- Autonomism has an open stance on the question of who or what is to be considered '*working class*'. Whereas Leninists have tended to favour the industrial proletariat, autonomists have regarded 'class composition' as a more complex matter. On some readings, students and housewives could be regarded as working class, particularly where such groups have joined in more general struggles for social and economic improvements. Holloway argues that since *everyone* feels the pain of capitalist exploitation in some way, we should all be regarded as revolutionary subjects – potentially at least.

- This leads, thirdly, to a *flexible stance on the nature of an anti-capitalist resistance* and its possible outcomes. Autonomists argue that it is the concentration of political and economic power that has to be combated, whether this power be in the hands of the capitalist class or representatives of the working class itself such as trade union leaderships or communist party bosses. Autonomists stress the self-organisation of ordinary people and thus the ability and capacity of ordinary people to lead resistances and develop post-capitalist alternatives. They point at instances such as the Piqueteros' taking over of factories in Argentina as evidence that ordinary men and women can effect transformation without a 'vanguard'.

- Historically, autonomism has favoured *decentralisation* and '*localisation*' over a transitionary dictatorship of the proletariat subordinating local struggles to the needs of the state. Any future society must be one based on communal autonomy, not state forms.

Autonomism stresses the facility ordinary people have for developing appropriate structures and forms of decision-making for themselves. This echoes the roots of the early (radical) critique of Bolshevism, which saw the latter as subordinating such forms of self-organisation to the needs of a vanguard party standing outside or beyond working class self-organisation. Autonomism might be thought of, then, as one way in which the libertarian aspects of Marxism can find expression.

Anarchism, or the art of not being 'in charge'

In the early nineteenth century revolutionaries and radicals of many different kinds were found under the same umbrella, namely The International Working Men's Association, otherwise known as the First International. It was set up in 1864 to co-ordinate working class resistance and the activities of various affiliated groups and parties. Marx, who quickly became the leading light of the International, envisaged it becoming a political party and a basis for securing power for the working class. This brought him into conflict with the many anarchists who were also involved in the International, many of whom followed Bakunin's critique of organised politics of the sort demanded by

Marx. Rupture followed. Bakunin and many other anarchists were expelled from (or left) the International. Anarchism and Marxism became the irreconcilable factions we see today. Although it is easily assumed that Marxism must be the more significant tendency, not least because communists established power in a number of countries, anarchism too has been a serious force in revolutionary and anti-capitalist politics. It has been capable of mobilising huge numbers despite – or perhaps because of – its lack of a developed ideology of the sort associated with Marxism. Anarchists were a major presence in the rebellions and uprisings of the late nineteenth and early twentieth centuries, particularly in Europe and Latin America. Anarchists were very much to the fore in the Russian Revolution and indeed helped establish Soviet power in the early years of the new regime. Once the libertarian goals of the Revolution were 'betrayed', anarchist leaders such as Nestor Makhno succeeded in capturing and controlling large tracts of territory from both the Bolsheviks and the counter-revolutionary White forces, proving a major thorn in the side to both. The high tide of anarchism as a political force was reached in the Spanish Civil War of the 1930s when the anarchists were perhaps the dominant force in the resistance ranged against Franco's fascists. This in turn reflected the popular base of anarchism particularly in the towns and villages of Andalucia, whose distance from Madrid offered a degree of autonomy and self-determination of the kind that collectivist variants of anarchism relish.

As for the contemporary political scene, anarchists are a vocal and visible part of many anti-capitalist initiatives. The Black Bloc, a loose coalition of militant anarchistic affinity groups, has been more or less ever-present at the larger demonstrations in the global North. Huge numbers of smaller groupings regularly participate in anti-capitalist protests as the ubiquity of anarchist papers such as *Class War*, *Total Liberty*, *Anarchy: the Journal of Desire Armed*, *Freedom*, *Here and Now*, *Organise!* (to name a small fraction) testify.

There are also many anarchist umbrella groupings operating internet-based networks such as CrimethInc based in North America, Anarkismo.net and Libcom.org offering discussion boards and classic and out-of-print materials.

Such a profusion of media is itself witness to the central fact about anarchism, which is that it is an umbrella term sheltering a staggeringly diverse range of political currents and groups. Yet the diversity of anarchism as a tradition and as a politics is rather different in nature to the diversity of the Marxist scene. Here it is less to do with *doctrinal* differences, and more to do with the very different reasons why it is possible to be opposed to the state in particular and centralised power or bureaucracy more generally. Anarchists do argue over which anarchist texts are the key ones; but one rarely hears or sees anarchist groups refer to themselves as say 'Bakuninite' or 'Tolstoyan' in the way Marxist groups term themselves 'Leninist', 'Maoist' or 'Trotskyist'. Indeed, to call oneself an 'anarchist' is to say very little of interest about oneself at all. One immediately needs to say what *kind* of anarchist, and in particular whether one is a collectivist or communist anarchist or an individualist or libertarian anarchist. Even with these distinctions we need to probe further, for there is a species of libertarian anarchist which is actually quite sympathetic towards capitalism, and thus not anti-capitalist at all. Those who follow the lead of classical American anarchist thinkers of the nineteenth century, such as Benjamin Tucker, Lysander Spooner or Josiah Warren, would probably find themselves sympathising with those *inside* the conference centre at the meetings of the WTO or World Bank defending capitalism against the attacks of the anti-capitalists outside. Indeed some of the more prominent American (libertarian) anarchists would no doubt argue that there is *too much* intervention in the world rather than not enough. For a glimpse of this other anarchism, just type in the names Ayn Rand, David Friedman or Murray Rothbard in *Google* and see what jumps out. *Pro*-capitalist anarchism is, as one might expect, particularly prevalent in the US where it feeds on the strong individualist and libertarian currents that have always been a part of the American political imaginary. To return to the point, however, there are individualist anarchists who are most certainly not anti-capitalist and there are those who may well be. Followers of Max Stirner, the nineteenth-century 'nihilistic egoist', would be among them, notwithstanding Marx's withering assault on his credentials to be considered a radical thinker. But we get to much more solid ground in considering the dominant tendency within anarchism, which is that of the collectivists or anarcho-communists. In what does their anti-capitalism consist?

Anarchists regard *the continuing existence of the state as an obstacle to the development of co-operative or communal existence*. Like Marxists, they generally agree that the state is an instrument of class rule, designed and maintained to secure private property rights, or, what amounts to the same, the private ownership of the means of production, the land, mines and factories. In this sense the critique of the state is often bound up with a critique of private property and of capitalism more generally. Bakunin, Proudhon and Peter Kropotkin, the three best known anarchists of the middle to late nineteenth century, were all anti-statists and anti-capitalists. Thereafter, however, anarchists tend to diverge strongly on what a post-capitalist society would be like, and in particular on what principle of social organisation would be appropriate to replace the capitalist market. Kropotkin, for example, was a keen advocate of 'mutualism', or the idea that co-operation is essentially innate to human nature. He envisaged forms of society that were reciprocal with people working together for the common good as opposed to working for profit or the market. This is the kind of anarchism favoured by, among others, Noam Chomsky who points to the co-operative basis of social life and thus the possibility of a non-antagonistic or mutualist global order. Proudhon, who developed a number of 'models', combined mutualist approaches with varieties of more or less strict egalitarianism.

In his most famous work, *What is Property?* (answer: 'theft!'), he argued that, since everyone is the product of society, everyone should receive equal shares from the social pot. On this logic poets would get the same pay as brain surgeons, as both are in some sense necessary in any society as well as being the product of it.

Others have argued for limited, i.e. non capitalist markets, or for gift economies in which people are encouraged to exchange without thought to equivalence. One of the more popular variants of recent times follow Tolstoy and Gandhi in arguing for a return to the subsistence economy, to the idea that we should grow only as much as we need to consume. This would be particularly so for the multiple green anarchisms that have sprung up since the 1970s. More generally, what tends to characterise collectivist anarchist approaches to post-capitalism is a perhaps healthy dose of optimism about human motivation, and also an undogmatic or non-doctrinal approach to issues of social organisation. Few anarchists are in favour of large scale social organisation, preferring instead a variety of local or regional solutions to decision-making, together with some form of loose federative structure to tackle issues of inter-communal interest such as transportation, pollution or infrastructure needs. A constant in all anarchist approaches is, nonetheless, that any such matters can be dealt with without the need for the state, for armed intervention or the threat of it. We can and do co-operate with each other; the problem is that capitalism prevents us from doing so more extensively than at present.

Means and ends

Some or all such approaches can be regarded as more or less in keeping with those of many varieties of Marxism, particularly the more autonomist kinds. It is for this reason that anarchists were able to sit alongside Marxists in the First International. Where anarchists have tended to depart from Marxists, sometimes radically so, is on the question of the means, of how one opposes the current system and advances to the new. The example of Bakunin is perhaps instructive in this respect. Marx's great rival in the First International, Bakunin had little difficulty recognising in Marx's thoughts on communism something akin to his own anarchism, which by contrast to Marx's was always more suggestive than firmly mapped out. Yet he consistently berated Marx on questions of organisation and strategy, and it is here that we find an echo of contemporary disputes between anarchists and Marxists. Bakunin's critique in the article 'Marxism, Freedom and the State' turned on three issues:

- the assumption that it is the experience of alienation or exploitation at the hands of the capitalist class that generated the desire to overcome capitalism;
- the identification of the working class as the agent of change to the exclusion of all others;
- the necessity for a state to guide the transition from capitalism to communism.

Bakunin opposed all three, setting a template for the more militant forms of anarchism we find in the contemporary anti-capitalist movement. He argued that:

- the desire to overcome oppression is a *universal* feature of human existence and thus to be found at least potentially in all individuals irrespective of class background or designation. Bakunin anticipated later neo-Marxists such as Herbert Marcuse, Toni Negri, Gilles Deleuze and Félix Guattari in pointing to the revolutionary potential of the 'riff-raff' or 'multitude' and thus opposed the privileged position accorded the working class in the Marxist revolutionary schema.
- the working class is as a *class* often amongst the *least* revolutionary elements of society, being content to agitate for better

working conditions, health and safety relations and enhanced pensions.

- the state cannot be deployed for revolutionary ends. Power has a tendency to corrupt even the most virtuous of revolutionaries.

The vitriol was not all directed one way. As Marx persistently argued, Bakunin's libertarian rhetoric was sharply at odds with his own recommendations for revolution which variously turned on the use of conspiratorial groups, assassinations, subterranean plots, subterfuge and revolutionary violence. Indeed Bakunin's reputation was permanently damaged by his association with the Russian terrorist Nechaev, the author of the notorious 'Catechism of a Revolutionary' which argued for indiscriminate use of terror to destabilise the existing state of affairs.

Such disputes and contradictions survive in contemporary relations between anarchists and Marxists, and indeed within anarchism itself. One of the most contentious issues as regards the latter is *the use of violence as an instrument of resistance*. Those advocating violence, sometimes known as 'Spikies', have clashed with the 'Fluffies', or those who advocate non-violent forms of direct action to advance the anti-capitalist cause. Within the spikier element there are those who distinguish between violence to property (such as McDonald's restaurants and other corporate property) and violence to persons, particularly the police and army, regarded by many militant anarchists as a legitimate target. In order to accommodate such differences of approach some anti-capitalist protests have been split into various different marches by the organisers.

The question of means and ends is hugely complex, and tends particularly in the anarchist movement to elicit the wildest possible variations, in turn emphasising the point that anarchism is a loose label rather than a consistent doctrine or ideology. Reflecting these differences it has to be accepted that there is a world of difference between the views of the Stirnerite 'egoist', the Kropotkinite collectivist and the Tolstoyan Christian anarchist.

This is part of the fascination as well as part of the frustration of anarchism historically. On the other hand, it would be wrong to imply that this diversity makes anarchism an ineffective or inconsequential body of ideas. As is evident, some of the most striking aspects of contemporary anti-capitalist initiatives have an anarchistic character. We could mention here both the *nature* and *form* of the World Social Forum, whose Charter insists that it reject the inheritance of representative politics, of political parties and vanguardism or leadership of a movement. In the WSF everyone has to be heard, and have her say. We see something similar in relation to the actions of the *Indignados* in Spain and the Occupy movement. No one can be represented or spoken for by some official, intellectual or otherwise privileged 'comrade'. Whilst this makes for necessarily 'anarchic' occasions and initiatives with little in the way of permanent monuments to celebrate, manifestos to rally behind or leaders to engage with, at the same time it is precisely the uncompromisingly collective nature of proceedings that to many anarchists imbues them with a legitimacy and standing that it would otherwise be difficult to match. To those who completely reject the possibility and desirability of doctrinal or ideological truth, the chaotic, free-form nature of such initiatives is the necessary price to be paid for its moral or ethical credibility as a counter-force to every kind of bureaucratic organisation whether capitalist or anti-capitalist in orientation. Living free from ideology and ideologues is what counts, and if this means having to put up with long meetings to bash out some sort of consensus on the way forward, then so be it. This is what a non-capitalist world *should* be like.

Thinking more concretely, there is now huge interest within anti-capitalist circles in the development of alternative economic systems springing up around both the developed and developing world, many of which have their origins in anarchist thought and activity. We could mention here the idea of alternative or parallel trading schemes that undercut or dispense with capitalistic forms of commerce, and also the efforts of many economists such as those associated with the 'participatory economics' or ParEcon initiative to develop trading schemes with a decidedly anarchistic air to them. Examples of the former include the use of labour notes whose units of denomination translate into labour hours. Within host areas, people are able to exchange products, goods and services without recourse to official currency and thus without recourse to banks, interest rates and the apparatus of capitalism. There are Local Exchange and Trading Schemes (LETS), barter schemes, and informal gift economies where people sign up to offer services or goods on a more or less benevolent basis. Such non-profit based forms of exchange are often very close to the kind of economic arrangements suggested by anarchists such as Proudhon and Kropotkin. Both argued that such schemes were a key to undermining capitalism and to establishing economic relations based on a different value system, one based on mutuality, trust and real equality. Such schemes are experiments in another way of living and organising social life. Their growing popularity across both developed and developing worlds demonstrates the continuing relevance of anarchistic proposals and practices notwithstanding the lack of agreement amongst anarchists themselves as to how to produce anarchism.

Deep, deeper, deepest 'green'

As we noted in the last chapter, one of the most important currents to have emerged out of the post-1968 realignment of politics is that of environmentalism or ecologism. The 'ism' appendage here should however not be taken to imply that there is some straightforward position to be unearthed or unpacked. Far from it. Green politics is a complex and sometimes conflicting amalgam of ideas that produces vociferous debates amongst its advocates. It is also worth bearing in mind that greens need not necessarily be anti-capitalist, and there are a great many who are not. These are regarded as 'light' greens as opposed to the 'deep' greens who frequently *are* anti-capitalist in orientation. Amongst the most important currents to note here are various American groups, in particular Earth First!, perhaps the largest and best known of the militant deep green collectives. We need to mention the various 'primitivist' groups who follow prominent thinkers such as John Zerzan, the author of *Future Primitive* and father figure to the *Green Anarchy* collective that also publishes the essays of other primitivists such as Eric Blair and Feral Faun. There are numerous eco-marxist, eco-feminist or eco-socialist groupings, though they lack the organisational visibility of groups like Earth First! Some of these are theoretically hybrid positions in that they combine elements from Marxism, autonomism or, more frequently, anarchism.

Many of these groups and collectives have been present at anti-capitalist carnivals, as well as the Earth summits and the various environmental protests they help organise. One should also bear in mind that there are many radical or anti-capitalist greens operating primarily within the official green parties (usually as 'fundis', as opposed to the 'realos' or realists), and also within many of the more prominent NGOs such as Greenpeace and Friends of the Earth. This is to say nothing about the wholly or largely unaffiliated activists who are the cornerstone of many of the direct action protests against environmental degradation and climate change across the developed and developing world. Indeed the contrast between green activism and Marxist activism is acute at this point. Many greens would see themselves primarily as 'doers', as activists working *directly* to prevent the harmful effects of capitalist production, rather than as working for an *organisation* ('the party') that will at some further point in time lead us to a post-capitalist future. From this point of view, their activism is often even more unofficial, non- or post-ideological and loose-limbed than those mentioned above.

The contrast with Marxist anti-capitalism is, however, much more acute at the level of ideology. Earlier in the chapter we noted that one of the distinguishing features of Marxism is not merely its acceptance of industrialisation and modernisation as requirements of socialism and thence communism, but its belief that without them the latter are impossible pipe dreams. Indeed Marx reserved some of his harshest criticism for 'romantic anti-capitalists' and 'utopian socialists' who imagined that a better society could be constructed before capitalism had run its course. Communism for Marx is a hyper-industrial society, a society that is able to satisfy needs, however expressed, whilst lowering the amount of time needed to produce necessary goods. This could only be achieved on the back of capitalism's relentless industrialising and modernising drive that in turn improved the productive potential available to humanity. It is partly for this reason that once it became apparent the much awaited global revolution had been 'postponed', the Bolshevik regime wasted little time in expending its energies and the energies of the Russian people on an effort to industrialise as rapidly as possible (Lenin:'Communism equals Soviet power plus *electrification*'). Industry was the key to socialism and the better life to come. From this point of view the emergence of the deep greens in the wake of 1968 was as a reaction to the super-industrialism shared by advocates of both capitalism and communism. As we noted in chapter 2, the 1973 Oil Crisis encouraged a rethinking of 'sustainability' and the limits to growth. At its most radical this rethinking prompted two currents of relevance for our purposes, one eco-centric and the other anthropo-centric.

Eco-centric thought, often strongly influenced by the work of James Lovelock, who developed the 'Gaia' hypothesis, stresses the necessity for regarding the Earth as prior to the humans who inhabit it. This notion of priority is not just temporal or chronological in the sense that the existence of the Earth is literally prior to the arrival of the human species, but philosophically and existentially prior as well. The Earth is in these senses 'first'. We need to abandon thinking of the Earth as a resource for us, as a common storehouse (as described in, for example, the Bible), or a gigantic warehouse that we can just use up at will. The Earth has rather to be thought of as a complex totality, of which we are merely a part, though a part with the potential to destroy as well as preserve life. From this point of view the objection to capitalism should already be clear. Capitalism perpetuates – indeed celebrates – the storehouse idea, seeing the world as a resource for exploitation for the purpose of private gain.

As a description of how capitalism works in practice, there is little to argue with in this image. As we noted in the first chapter, the effect of competition, particularly intense competition, is to drive out considerations of the *implicit* worth or value of resources such as rainforests or rare species. To the capitalist, such resources have a value insofar as they can be exploited and sold in the market place. Rainforests have a value primarily as timber, which in turn can be sold for a profit in the global market place for wood products. To eco-centric activists, capitalism has to be combated in order to reverse the ethical priority of the market over the Earth. Whatever damages or threatens the Earth must be challenged, which in the case of Earth First! means direct action against loggers or timber workers, if necessary by 'monkey-wrenching' – the dismantling of machinery. It also implies the deployment of a moral calculus of a particularly controversial kind, for what is also implicit in the eco-centric position is a more or less egalitarian stance as between the worth of different species. It is *Earth* first, not humanity first, which in turn implies that what is natural is good. Thus should nature offer solutions to population growth such as AIDS or monsoons or plagues, then nature should be allowed to take its course. Indeed why should the mosquito carrying the plague be regarded as of lesser value at all, if it is accepted that all species have the same value? This is an extreme working out of a certain kind of eco-centric logic found in such groups; but it shows, firstly, the undeniably radical nature of what is on offer, and, secondly, the degree to which the world would have to change or be remade in order to give life to the ideology. Necessary measures would include:

- cessation of the exploitation of natural resources in favour of a harmonious relationship between humanity and the planet;
- end of production for profit in favour of de-industrialised solutions that prioritise the preservation of the wilderness;
- end of state-centric solutions to questions of organisation, infrastructure, collective provision of all kinds. Social organisation to be non-hierarchical, non-dominating, de-centralised.

Anthropo-centric approaches that are more 'humanistic' in orientation can be just as radical as eco-centric ones. Primitivism, which has risen in prominence amongst environmental anti-capitalists in recent years, argues for a complete rejection of industry and technology and thus for a return to 'primitive', even Stone Age, forms of life. Here again the object of the critique is the industrialism of both capitalism and communism, both of which assert the necessity for progress and the utilisation of technology for human benefit. Such benefits are explicitly queried by Zerzan who follows a line of counter-Enlightenment theorists such as Tolstoy and Marcuse in seeing us as enslaved to the technological machine. In his view, if we are serious about constructing a post-capitalist society built on genuine equality, and the obliteration of hierarchy and bureaucracy in the name of a richness of existence, then we need to recognise the pernicious and debilitating effect of industry – indeed civilisation – itself ('For the Destruction of Civilisation – For Reconnection to Life!'). In this sense Zerzan is unafraid of the charge that supporters of capitalism have often made against anti-capitalist radicals, which is that in opposing economic growth or development they would necessarily forfeit the advantages that come from competition in terms of the trickle down of technological benefits such as new medicines, or faster computers. For him the advantages are hollow and illusory compared to a life restored to the wild.

Moving away from the radical end of the spectrum, there are many more moderate though still anti-capitalist variations on both the eco-centric and anthropo-centric positions that have their supporters. Indeed it would be an exaggeration to imply that ultra-radical positions such as those of Earth First! and the primitivists are necessarily dominant amongst environmentalists despite their high profile. Looking at eco-activist materials what becomes apparent is that there is a tendency to avoid grandiose ideological positions altogether in favour of a pragmatic, and non-ideological stance in relation to the question of post-capitalist alternatives. A defence of the concept of sustainability as against the excesses of capitalism in its relentless quest to transform the planet into exchange values is evidently enough to sustain a variety of radical currents and activisms. Indeed, environmentalists often hitch their wagon to traditions of thought such as Marxism, anarchism and feminism in an effort to refine both the nature of the critique of capitalism offered and the kind of world that they wish to see lib-erated or created. Yet, what seems clear is that radical environmen-tal activism is primarily *practical* and *immediate* for many of its most enthusiastic followers. There are many ways in which environmen-talists can achieve a sense of worth and satisfaction in the here and now, for example through blocking building programmes, lobby-ing on behalf of an endangered species, saving a forest or a green space, hosting street carnivals to 'reclaim the streets' or critical mass bike rides to underscore the necessity for sustainable transport. In this sense even radical environmentalists can at times sound curi-ously *apolitical*, as if *all* that mattered was saving the turtles or the rainforests. To those who care deeply about such issues, this may *indeed* be all that matters, in the same way that a mother without food for her children may well be completely unconcerned about where the food has come from or how it was manufactured.

What the above indicates is that there is something very particular about green radicalism as opposed to, say, Marxist or anarchist activism. This is that it is predominantly *non-* or *post-ideological*. Many greens are happy to say that if you want an argument against capitalism, then just look at the state of the world, look at what capitalism *does*. As we noted in the last chapter, it is this resolutely non-ideological aspect of environmental activism that is one of its great attractions for those wearied by what seems like the internal wrangling and self-serving of other kinds of radicalism. But what it means is that radical environmentalism tends to concentrate more on what is wrong with the present than on how the present is to be changed for the better. Or else, it seems dimly suggestive of something else such as anarchism or socialism, in which case it might with some legitimacy be asked what exactly is 'green' about green anti-capitalism? On the other hand if this implies that there is a strong commonality between, say, anarchists and radical greens – as perhaps embodied in the work of Kropotkin, E.F. Schumacher or William Morris – then this has the considerable merit of keeping lines of communication and alliance open, in turn permitting the forms of broad-based, '(dis)organised' action that groups such as Reclaim the Streets and Critical Mass have promoted with considerable impact over the past decade or so.

On the face of it a chapter on contemporary revolutionary positions that covers red, black and green anti-capitalisms might be thought to more or less exhaust the subject. It does not. One of the most obvious omissions is that of feminism. Many feminists will no doubt look at the male author of the book and say 'typical'. In defence, many feminists themselves note the difficulty of identifying a distinctly feminist post-capitalism, as opposed to the numerous varieties of Marxist feminism, anarcho-feminism and eco-feminism acting and interacting within each sub-radicalism.

This is not to say that women play anything like a lesser role in the anti-capitalist protests. Far from it. It is clear that women are every bit as engaged in anti-capitalist initiatives as are men, in some cases more so. It is to say that radical anti-capitalist feminism has tended to annex itself – or become annexed to – sub-radicalisms. There are numerous reasons why this might be the case. One suggestion is that with the fragmentation of the feminist movement itself in the late 1970s and 1980s, many radical feminists moved down the 'single-issue' road, embarking on campaigns against various legal, political, economic or social inequalities. Another is that feminists sought common cause with others to advance the interests of women beneath red, black or green umbrellas. Whatever the case, it will be interesting to see whether a radical anti-capitalist feminism does develop to take its place alongside the sub-groupings we have in fact covered.

Ya Basta!: a brief excursus on Marcos and 'Zapatismo'

A different problem is created by the case of the Zapatistas, whom we have not so far covered in our brief review of radical anti-capitalisms. As is probably obvious, there is a strong temptation for political theorists like myself to subordinate what emerges today to ideas that existed in the past, sometimes the far-flung past. Contemporary anarchists (say) sound a lot like anarchists of the past and so one is tempted to assume they must in some strong sense *be* the same, when they might not be. The same is true for Marxism which has a similarly strong link to the past; rather less so environmentalism, which is much more a product of the contemporary world, notwithstanding those echoes of the past. With the Zapatistas, however, even know-it-all theorists have to recognise that something novel has been advanced, even if (yes) one can hear the occasional echo. They are clearly not

Marxists, not anarchists and not environmentalists. Nor is their stance some muddy mixture of all three, or some sublime *Über-*radicalism that somehow takes the best or most significant elements and transcends them all. There is something *new* about Zapatismo that demands that it be treated for what it is. We should also note that the Zapatistas occupy a place in the affections of anti-capitalists that other groups and positions do not. Marxists argue with anarchists who argue with environmentalists, who argue with reformists and so forth. Indeed, despite the common cause, enmities, some of them ancient, still flicker beneath the surface of exchanges between camps, reminding us of the difficulty involved in reconciling different philosophies and world views to the same political cause. But when it comes to the Zapatistas, it is noticeable that at the very least there is considerable respect not only for what they have done, but more intriguingly what they represent. Who are the Zapatistas and what makes them unique?

To begin with some context, the Zapatistas are the latter day inheritors of the mantle of Emiliano Zapata, one of the leaders of the Mexican revolution of 1910. Zapata's programme was a simple yet radical one. He wanted to challenge the ownership of land which then as now was monopolised by a small number of families, who had inherited their vast riches from the Spanish *Conquistadores*. Zapata was ultimately unsuccessful and indeed he was later murdered by conservative forces led by Colonel Guajardo. The dream of land redistribution nevertheless lived on and was later taken up by an insurgent guerrilla force, the Ejército Zapatista de Liberación Nacional (EZLN) or Zapatistas. A seemingly ramshackle group of students, intellectuals, radicals and indigenous peasant rebels, the Zapatistas emerged from the jungle of the Chiapas region in 1994 within hours of the signing of the NAFTA agreement, hounding the Mexican federal forces from the region. Since 1994 Mexico's leaders have seemed unsure about how to respond to the situation, oscillating between violent incursion in the Chiapas region and offering talks to placate the troublesome insurgents. As a result a precarious 'autonomous zone' of some forty or so villages has subsisted beyond or outside federal control. This is to say that within Mexico, a relatively industrialised country of one hundred million people, the Zapatistas were able to establish an autonomous area governed by an entirely different set of principles and norms, indeed a different philosophy, to the rest of the country. It is difficult to think of parallels in what is now supposed to be a 'global village' dominated by corporate interests. It is difficult to think too of a parallel for Subcomandante Insurgente Marcos, the Zapatista leader who since 1994 has orchestrated communications between the Zapatistas and the outside world. It is Marcos who has translated an otherwise homespun and admittedly pragmatic set of principles into what is now termed 'Zapatismo', something that is part poetry, part philosophy, part rebel folklore. What then is Zapatismo, and what is its significance for the matters under review?

As Marcos describes the situation, he left Mexico City as an impatient and idealistic student full of Marxian and quasi-Marxian ideas about how to liberate the indigenous peoples and embark on a revolution that would sweep away Mexico's creaking political establishment. Yet having made it to the mountains and jungles of the Chiapas and telling the people he met what it was that was required for their emancipation, he found himself listening to what it was that they were telling him. He realised that they knew everything they needed to know about how they should live, how they wanted to live, and thus that they had no need for his advice let alone his leadership. What they lacked was the *means* by which they could live their lives according to their own needs, interests and traditions. From this simple reversal of roles, Marcos seems to have evolved an entire non-philosophy based on 'listening' rather than 'speaking for'. This already sounds rather obscure, so for the sake of getting clear about what is novel here, let's go back and recall some of what we have just been covering above.

Recall the theme of the chapter. We are discussing radical ideas about emancipation, liberation, freedom. In particular we have been contrasting ideologies. We said at the outset that possessing an ideology is like possessing an image or painting of how the world should look. Those who possess an ideology want the rest of us to see that the painting is in some important sense true, that it accurately pictures a world most if not all of us would recognise as desirable if not ideal. We might for some reason not see it that way yet; but we will, or we will once we begin to see things clearly. This puts the possessor of an ideology in a privileged position – but also an invidious one – vis-à-vis those who are yet to be convinced. He or she needs them to see the truth of the picture in order to bring the picture about; he or she needs to convince them of the truth or desirability of the underlying analysis and account of how the world could be better. Failing this, then the canvas remains just that, a picture or image, and not a *reality*. In order to change the world people need to be *mobilised* behind a set of ideas.

To return to Marcos's tale, what becomes obvious is that he saw that what the indigenous people wanted was not a new ideology, but release *from* an ideology, namely neoliberalism. The Zapatista revolt was in this sense a revolt *against* neoliberalism in the form of the NAFTA agreement which would make the life of Mexico's poor even more miserable than it already was. Yet more than this, he began to see that the issue was not just about neoliberal ideology, but ideology more generally, even revolutionary ideology. What struck him was that the peoples of the Chiapas *already knew* how they would like to live. They simply wanted to run their own affairs rather than being pushed around by outsiders. This did not just mean the big landowners, the Mexican federal government, or the big corporations who would now be unleashed on the basis of the NAFTA agreement.

Outsiders also meant revolutionaries, indeed those with the very best interests of the peasants at heart. Those like Marcos who were sensitive to what it was that the peasants actually wanted, as opposed to what it was that they *should* want, saw that their job was to do nothing more than ensure that what the peasants themselves wanted to see happen happened. In short he self-consciously gave up the position of the revolutionary, the ideologist, the intellectual with a pre-packaged solution or idea of how the peasants should live. One of his communiqués in 2002 was entitled 'I shit on all the Revolutionary Vanguards of this Planet', underpinning the extent to which Marcos had not merely broken from the revolutionary tradition but had begun to see it as an obstacle to the development of resistance. The Zapatistas thus enacted a non- or post-ideological form of politics centred on guaranteeing a space within which the indigenous peoples could organise their own affairs and indeed organise the affairs of the Zapatistas whose own rationale was now nothing more – though certainly nothing less – than ensuring the integrity of the autonomous zone itself. What are the ramifications of such a stance in terms of what we are considering here?

Zapatismo and post-ideology

As a post-ideological politics Zapatismo effectively renounces the superstructure of expectations that have informed political philosophy since Plato invented the Philosopher Kings in 400 BC. This is to say that it has forsaken the idea that knowledge or understanding can give a superior insight into issues concerning how we should live, and thus that, for example, I as a political theorist with thirty or so years' worth of heavy reading behind me, have the right or the role to legislate on behalf of others. It means that what the intellectuals or the vanguards say is simply one set of views to be considered (or not) alongside everyone else's views – no matter how ridiculous, incomprehensible, outlandish or outrageous the latter may seem. Everyone's voice has in this sense equal weight and an equal right to be heard. If this sounds quite a lot like a certain kind of democratic liberalism, then in a sense it is. But Marcos insistently poses the questions: which liberal is it that actually *wants* the unmediated voice to help decide? Which liberal thinks that voices are more important than structures, institutions and constitutions? Which liberal wants our voice to be heard on every matter facing the community, whether it be the kind of crops to be sown or the direction of military strategy? Which liberal is *really* prepared to hear everyone's voice, without the convenience of representatives to give sense or 'wisdom' to them? Certainly not the neoliberals. The problem is that liberalism *in practice* is quite a different proposition to democratic liberalism *in theory*, which in turn explains the success of liberalism in establishing itself as the dominant or hegemonic idea of the modern world. They *say* they are listening, but are they *really*?

As it pans out in practice, Zapatismo looks a lot less like liberalism and a lot more like direct democracy. Within the zone, for example, the forty communes or villages exercise power, as Marcos puts it, meaning that the villages run their own affairs on the basis of discussions held at village or commune level. Inter-communal or zonal affairs are handled by 'Clandestine Revolutionary Indigenous Committees' (CCRIs) elected on direct democratic principles. But even the meetings of the CCRIs are open to any and all *compañeros* who wish to make themselves heard. Decision-making appears to follow the principle, if not of unanimity then of overwhelming consensus, with dissenting voices entertained until such time as general agreement is reached. This makes for long, indeed sometimes interminable, meetings; but the feeling seems to be that this is the necessary price for reaching outcomes found satisfactory to the communities themselves. It should be added that the Zapatistas are themselves answerable to the CCRIs, with military strategy worked out by a similar process of deliberation. Yet what is noticeable is that despite the clearly anarchistic basis of decision-making, anarchists have been amongst those most ambivalent in their reaction to the Zapatistas. Why could this possibly be? Isn't this anarchy 'in action' and thus a cause for celebration? It is here that we begin to see how Zapatismo is different as an approach to revolutionary politics to what has gone before.

The dilemma for anarchists, Marxists and others committed to a given vision of how the world should look should be apparent. This is that, to recall, Marcos and the Zapatistas are not committed to any particular vision of the world. As they made startlingly clear in one of their earliest pronouncements, they are committed 'to the creation of a world in which *all* worlds are possible'. They are not committed to anarchy, to direct democracy, to the socialisation of production or to any model or blueprint for human happiness as such. Nor are they committed to peasant farming or the CCRIs in principle. They are committed to getting rid of the grip of one particular ideology, neoliberalism, so that other visions can circulate, breathe and come to be discussed by the collective. They are committed to giving everyone a voice, and a stake in the world. In this sense they are committed to something much less elaborate than an ideology but, as they put it, to the simple values of 'dignity' and 'respect', and this in turn means *not presuming to know in advance* what it is that the voice wants or needs. It presumes that one is going to *listen* to the voices, not ignore them. As we noted above, Zapatismo is in this sense an anti-philosophy or anti-doctrine. It has no recommendations to make, no final answers to the great problems of life. Zapatismo concerns the creation of *autonomous space* rather than *ideas about autonomy*. It seeks to create spaces or to enlarge those that already exist within which people can exercise their own autonomy. In this sense it finds itself in direct opposition to another spatial political project, namely neoliberalism. Neoliberals argue in favour of an enlargement of the *sphere* of free trade, bringing the benefits of the market to the globe. Neoliberalism appears as a morally and ethically neutral project. Its spokespeople say it is 'beyond ideology', that it is only concerned with allowing people access to the market and thus to the means by which their own dreams and needs can be fulfilled. Economic globalisation, we are told, is about creating a sphere of free activity; but not telling us what to do with it. What seems evident is that the power of Zapatismo lies in this ability to match the discursive power of neoliberalism and free market ideology. The rhetoric of space it employs is a rhetoric in which the freedom to decide remains intact, the freedom to choose, the freedom to be heard. The difference is, as seems clear from the experience of the Chiapas, is that it is not *just* rhetoric; they mean it.

If all this seems impossibly utopian and other-worldly, then it is. This is one of its charms, and why so many have invested so many hopes and fears in the continued ability of the Zapatistas to hold the Mexican federal forces at bay. What such investments paper over is the problem of advancing a post-ideological project of the kind represented by Zapatismo. It is only fair to enumerate what such problems might amount to so that we get a sense of why it is that more ideologically committed groups have a problem with it. Such groups argue:

- A post-ideological stance is politically *disabling*. It means that activists are required to give up offering a positive alternative account of how the world might look in favour of a *negative* or oppositional stance against something else (i.e. neoliberalism). The force of the message is *reactive*, not active as many radicals think it should be.
- Activists are prey to the immediate, perhaps uncritical wishes of their constituency. One of the tensions in the Zapatista zone has, for example, been the place of women in decision-making and, indeed, in social life more generally. Many women have been an active presence in the struggle, yet many men wish their wives and partners would stay at home playing the part of the traditional mother. This in turn creates a tension between the EZLN which itself has embraced the role of women in the struggle and some of the men who are

unwilling to let go of their traditional views. Lacking a doctrine or clear ideology inevitably leaves the Zapatistas open to the charge that they are arbitrarily siding with one part of the community against another, without the mandate of either.

- Renouncing a leadership function for themselves makes Zapatismo itself look like a localised solution for a local problem, and thus in turn one living on borrowed time. As they put it themselves, they are not interested in 'capturing power', only ensuring that the people of the Chiapas are able to 'exercise' it. Is this then to say that they are not interested in extending the struggle to the rest of the region or to the rest of Mexico – or the rest of the world? If so, why should the political elites in Mexico City be worried? No leadership function means no threat of the Zapatistas breaking out of their zone to nurture, support and help neighbouring insurgents. 'Let them *have* the Chiapas'.

Such criticisms are rarely offered with the purpose of belittling the Zapatista achievement, though of course Marcos is surely entitled to respond in appropriately robust fashion ('I shit on all the Revolutionary Vanguards' …). What such queries perhaps highlight is that the advancement of a non-or post-ideological position is not without its own difficulties, as if merely renouncing ideology as such would somehow make it easier to develop a post-capitalist alternative. As is clear, it won't. Or at least it won't in all cases and in all places. What the Zapatista case tells us, however, is that a post or non-ideological position *can* be enough for a significant and effective kind of resistance, particularly where 'the enemy' is clearly defined and perceived in such terms. Here lie some clues to the Zapatistas' success in their own zone:

- They are reacting to widely, almost universally perceived injustices, in this case the retention of land and resources by non-indigenous families and corporate interests.

- They are seeking to defend or restore a way of life against centuries of abuse and maltreatment at the hands of settlers.
- They seek to re-enact practices of decision-making that were widely presumed to work before they were overturned in the process of the creation of the settler state.

In short, they are defending an indigenous cultural practice and way of life against that of the Mexican political and economic elites, albeit with some modifications to ensure that certain concerns are respected or taken on board, such as the position of women. It will be interesting to reflect on the degree to which such conditions are operative elsewhere.

Conclusion

This has been a long discussion and we need to think about what, if anything, has been learned. I mentioned at the start of chapter 3 that there is general acceptance that there is no anti-capitalist movement as such, only at best a 'movement of movements'. I also suggested that underneath the umbrella lay diverse, plural and conflicting accounts of how the anti-capitalist resistance should proceed. What should be obvious, having overviewed a sample of some of the currents on offer, is the sheer degree of plurality and thus the ever-present scope for conflict between the different radical currents. Indeed it is probably true to say that the only matter they all agree on is that capitalism should be opposed. *How* it should be opposed, by what means and to what ends, is the subject of profound and sometimes bitter dissensus. Looking over the accounts of libertarian Marxism, autonomism, anarchism, certain kinds of green radicalism and towards Zapatismo, there are nonetheless definite points of contact and coalescence. These might be summarised as follows:

- Economic affairs need to be *re-politicised*: made subject to the needs, wants and desires of both consumers *and* producers.

- People need to be *re-empowered*: given the opportunity to take part in vital decisions regarding their own affairs.
- Power needs to be *re-localised*: power should be closer to the people, not abstracted away to national governments or global structures unaccountable to those below.
- Decisions need to be *re-popularised*: elite rule should give way to forms of interaction that permit the circulation or flow of decision-making capacity amongst ordinary people themselves.

Quite a lot of this concerns the *form* that power or decision-making should take, rather than the substance or the outcomes. If there is a common theme to both radical and reformist anti-capitalism then it is the *primacy of the political* over the purely economic and thus the need to recuperate power from those who have annexed it through support for a depoliticised free market. We need more politics, not less. We need more discussion, more occasions to participate than are currently granted by the 'new rulers of the world'. From Tahrir Square through the movement of the *Indignados* to the Occupy movement, the demand is less the overthrow of capitalism than the establishment of 'real' or 'true' democracy, a democracy in other words that is not in thrall to the IMF, to the World Bank, to elites, bankers, development agencies, but a democracy for ordinary people, a democracy 'for the rest of us'. But how is politics to be reborn? How can such an intuitively felt observation, shared by so many, become the basis for a global movement that is *effective* as well as noisy?

5

The future(s) of anti-capitalism: problems and perspectives

So we've learned a lot about anti-capitalist ideas. In particular, we've learned that there are some very significant differences between those who self-identify as anti-capitalist and those who are sometimes called 'anti-capitalist' by others – such as the press, or those defending capitalism, markets, or globalisation. But what a lot of those interested in anti-capitalism also want to know about is the anti-capitalist *movement*, which today is also termed the global justice movement. Since the Zapatista insurrection of 1994 and then Seattle in 1999 political commentary has been full of analyses of the movement or 'movement of movements'. Much speculation was subsequently generated concerning how the movement would develop and what its impact might be. Some anticipated it would develop into a fully-fledged political party with a detailed programme capable of mobilising ordinary people behind an alternative to neoliberal capitalism. Others remained sceptical and indeed fearful about such an eventuality. They didn't want the movement of movements to congeal into a 'vertical' traditional revolutionary party. However, there is very little evidence to suggest that an anti-capitalist movement of *this kind* is emerging or that it will emerge any time in the foreseeable future. On the contrary, as I discuss in the first part of this chapter, there are serious obstacles to the development of such a movement. Much more likely is the development of a new style of what I term 'resonant' politics that breaks firmly with the legacy of previous movements, but which nonetheless can be regarded as 'anti-capitalist'.

What happened to the 'anti-capitalist movement'?

In the decade following the Seattle protests of 1999, there was a great deal of activity that pointed at the emergence of a serious political force: the 'anti-capitalist movement', 'anti-globalisation movement' or 'global justice movement'. Among the more obvious signs were:

- *an intensification of well-organised and co-ordinated protests, demonstrations and global 'days of action'* timed to coincide with the key meetings of the institutions of global governance, such as the WTO, the G7 and G20. These protests were also 'convergences': they brought together the 'movement of movements', providing opportunities to share analyses, tactics, strategies.
- the development of the *World Social Forum* in 2001, designed to create an 'open space for dialogue' concerning the nature of the injustices perpetrated by neoliberalism and opportunities to discuss how best to overcome them. Very quickly this initiative proliferated forums in what became known as the 'Social Forum process' at the continental, regional, national and local levels. There were also forums designed to bring together indigenous people and other groups and communities whose interests could not be encapsulated in geographical terms.
- the consolidation of *autonomous networks* such as ATTAC, Dissent!, nadir.org, Struggle and a great variety of groups

protesting against specific injustices such as Students Against Sweatshops. These networks provided the organisational basis and energy for many of the protests and events taking place. They also provided the most obvious means whereby the numerous *autonomous initiatives* designed to recapture space, territory or resources threatened by the encroachment of neoliberalism could be tied together for solidarity and support. We've already discussed the case of the Zapatistas; and there are many other significant autonomous resistances such as the Narmada Dam protests, the Piqueteros movement in Argentina, and quasi-permanent peasant and indigenous rebellions in areas such as West Bengal, various parts of China, West Papua and South Africa, to mention but a few.

Together these initiatives seem to indicate the coming together of otherwise diverse groupings to create something more unified: a movement devoted to combating neoliberalism. However, and with the benefit of a great deal of hindsight, that judgement appears not merely premature, but unrealistic. What happened?

The perils of 'movementism'

As we noted in chapter 2, few people were talking about the 'anti-capitalist movement' or the 'anti-globalisation movement' before the Seattle protests of 1999. This brought together trade unionists, community activists and those protesting either at specific injustices or because of a more general sense of anger about the behaviour of the developed world and its treatment of the developing world. The 'Battle of Seattle', as it came to be known, provided televisual evidence that a new movement had been born. In the aftermath of Seattle there was a great outpouring of analysis in the media about what all of this meant. But of course this wasn't an isolated event. It was only the beginning of a sequence of protests across the developed world that included demonstrations in Genoa, Prague, Evian, Québec, Gleneagles and so forth. A pattern had been set. Groups planned a variety of actions to coincide with the meeting of global elites, and camps would be set up with all sorts of educational, learning and community spaces where activists could assemble to discuss how best to combat neoliberalism.

Many of these marches, protests and initiatives were very successful on their own terms. This is to say that they provided a focal point for activists who might not have had wider contact with concerned citizens or groups who shared some if not all of their aims and objectives. The protests were mobilising occasions. They enabled people to learn and share experiences in an intense environment which heightened the sense of a great deal being at stake. They also seemed to matter in tangible as well as intangible ways. Elites certainly gave the impression that they were concerned about these protests, and this served to reinforce the feeling that the stakes were high. Huge numbers of police and military personnel were used to protect conference centres, hotels and the participants themselves from the protesters. The protests tapped into popular sentiment and in their own ways affected the climate of opinion, such that elites had to be responsive to the concerns articulated by the protesters.

So for a while it seemed that protests and demonstrations were an effective way of bringing activists together and influencing the actions and policies of global elites. Here, quite tangibly, was 'the movement'. However, even within the movement there were those who expressed scepticism about such an emphasis being given to what had become a mobile carnival of protests and demonstrations – or 'serial protesting' as Naomi Klein aptly put it. Alex Callinicos, to take one notable example, offered a critique of what he termed 'movementism', which he equated to the belief that protests and demonstrations would displace the need for more durable forms of organisation, for the development of a programme and ultimately for capturing power *from* elites as opposed to merely *influencing them* in the direction of more just or equitable policies. He predicted, presciently as it turned out, that once the initial wave of energy and enthusiasm for protests had begun to wane, the shortcomings of this approach would be revealed and that in its stead would be left recrimination and few victories. What Callinicos neglects in his argument is that one of the reasons why activists focused on protests and demonstrations is because 'party building' seemed such a tired formula. Protests were the antidote to the Leninist 'cure' as far as many disaffiliated activists were concerned. On the other hand, it is certainly true that much of the momentum went out of summit protests over the course of the first decade of the twenty-first century. This was so for several reasons, which it is worth recounting to get a sense of the changing context in which anti-capitalist initiatives took place.

Firstly, what became obvious was the *mounting cost to individuals and groups* of taking part in major demonstrations. As part of the War on Terror unleashed in the wake of the 9/11 al-Qaeda attacks, most states had invested significantly in intelligence services, counter-terrorism initiatives, surveillance capacity and police and army training to combat threats to 'civil security'. This was justified by reference to the threat of attack from religious extremists. But 'threat' is an elastic term that can be used to encompass a range of 'extremists' who seem to represent a threat to law and order. Many of these techniques were now deployed against those engaged in anti-capitalist protests and demonstrations. It became familiar for protesters in, for example, the UK to be confronted by a squad of police officers – the Forward Intelligence Team (FIT) – brandishing cameras to record the faces of all those engaged in a protest. Such overt displays of policing are designed to fulfil two functions. Firstly, they demonstrate to the public that protests are considered by authorities on the same continuum as more violent or terroristic activities. Secondly, they are designed to intimidate participants. Making protestors the subject of overt surveillance is a Draconian reminder of 'who is in charge'. The idea is to ramp up the personal cost of being engaged in such activities, deterring ordinary people who may wish to demonstrate their displeasure at government policy or the actions of global elites. This leaves behind a rump of more militant activists who can more easily be monitored and controlled.

If we think back to the characteristics of the Seattle protests, the implications of this kind of intimidatory policing are clear. What impressed about Seattle was precisely that it was not a protest composed exclusively of militants, or experienced protesters. Many of the protesters were trade unionists, teachers, civil servants, all manner of people who wanted to voice their disapproval of the WTO. Many such participants would be put off participating in protest if they thought that their careers, their credit rating with the bank, their mortgages and their life chances would be threatened as a result. Yet with the ramping up of the security response to protests, this is exactly what was at stake. As became clear, the climate in many advanced democracies became decidedly unsympathetic towards protests and demonstrations. Fewer people participated in them, leaving those who did with the feeling that the tide had turned and thus that other strategies were needed. By the end of the first decade of the twenty-first century, Seattle-style protests against international organisations had become relatively low key affairs, attended largely by the very committed. Of course soon after the waning of summit protests Occupy emerged to re-engage issues similar to those of the summit protests. But if anything Occupy represents a further strengthening of the symptoms of which Marxists such as Callinicos and Žižek are critical. Summit protests and convergences were, after all, often used as recruiting grounds by far left groups and their umbrella groups such as 'Globalise Resistance'. Occupy, however, has proved much more resistant to the attempts of activists to be incorporated in such fashion. Indeed Occupy might be said to be as much an *anti-Leninist* initiative as an anti-capitalist one. By steadfastly refusing to develop demands, a programme, a manifesto, offices, leaders and so on, Occupy exemplifies in its permanently intransigent stance of refusal the very logic of the political – both of a mainstream kind and an oppositional kind.

The spectacular rise and fall of the World Social Forum

Just as symbolic as summit protests in terms of generating the sense of a movement beginning to coalesce globally to confront neoliberalism was the creation of the World Social Forum (WSF) in 2001. The brainchild of the Brazilian Workers Party (PT) led by future President Lula da Silva and the editorial board of the French progressive journal *Le Monde diplomatique*, the WSF was designed to create a space in which diverse groups and movements could come together to share their analysis and formulate strategies to resist capitalism. The first edition, held in Porto Alegre in Brazil, was an astonishing success. The organisers had planned the event for several thousand participants, but estimated that around 60,000 showed up. Initially a one-off event, it was clear to the organisers that there was an appetite for an annual event at the very least. Subsequent editions attracted hundreds of thousands of participants and engaged the attentions of the world's media and indeed of the elites. Something extraordinary had been born: the institutionalisation of an event whose avowed purpose was to stimulate discussion concerning how best to resist neoliberalism. This success was amplified more or less immediately with the proliferation of forums across the world. There were various continental forums, regional and national forums, and many local and city forums as well. For a while it seemed that the social forum process would provide the institutional as well as symbolic locus for resistance to capitalism.

Notwithstanding the astonishing success of the forum in drawing thousands of people into a conversation about the future of the world's poor and oppressed, criticisms from both within the forum process and without began to emerge. Critics worried about the governance of the forum process itself, about who was running the forums and what their agenda might or might not be. Certainly little thought seemed to have been given as to how to make the structure of the forum process accountable or democratic. Perhaps the organisers felt there was no need to do so, given the characteristics of the forum, which as we recall involve creating a 'space for dialogue', as opposed to creating a new political party or movement that would represent the needs, interests and wishes of those within it. Nonetheless the result was an ominously opaque decision-making structure, led by an International Committee dominated by members of the Brazilian PT, white middle-class activists from Scandinavia and representatives of various NGOs who underwrote the considerable costs of the WSF. As a result, the organising committee failed to look even vaguely representative of those who attended the forum process. Other criticisms followed. The 2004 WSF, which was held in Mumbai, was attacked for excluding various castes and ethnicities from its organising committee and deliberations. At the 2007 WSF held in Nairobi, protests were held around the WSF venue concerning the cost of entry. Events there quickly took on a surreal twist, for no sooner were locals granted free access than protests took place under the banner 'Free Everything'. The gesture was symbolic of the paradoxes of the WSF – an initiative led by often middle-class white people from comfortable backgrounds organising an event at which the needs and interests of the very poor were to be debated, but without the means of allowing the poor to participate in a meaningful way.

Paradoxes such as these abounded at the WSF. What, for example, of the Zapatistas, the poster movement for many activists, locked out of the official proceedings of the WSF because the Charter forbids the involvement of 'paramilitary' groups engaged in armed struggle? As it turned out the Zapatistas did attend some of the WSF proceedings, as and when they could; but of course they did so on a 'non-official basis' and confined themselves to activities outside the perimeter of the WSF itself. What of the WSF's commitment to forms of dialogue untainted by political parties or political organisations? As we have heard, the WSF was created and largely paid for by a political party: the Brazilian PT. What of the Caracas WSF of 2006, which was funded to large degree by Hugo Chavez? One could go on.

More predictably, the organised left began to air its own conviction that the WSF was little more than what it in fact was: a talking shop. An attempt was made by some prominent Marxists, Samir Amin and François Houtart, to prompt consideration of transforming the WSF into a political movement (the 'Bamako Appeal') so that it could begin to organise resistance in a much more meaningful and direct fashion. That appeal fell largely on deaf ears.

In the end, the demise of the WSF was not really due to any strategic or tactical mistake on behalf of the organisers, who were only guilty of putting on an event that could never satisfy the demands of every participant within it. Its very success proved ultimately to be the source of its own decline. From having started out as an idea of bringing people together in spaces to discuss shared experiences and future strategies, it had become an uncontrollable monster, too expensive for the modest social movements behind it to mount, too deliberative to satisfy the needs of those who called for action as opposed to dialogue, too ephemeral to satisfy the hard heads and the global revolutionary elites. Momentum waned. The energy dissipated, and just as soon as this extraordinary initiative had been created, so it seemed to all but disappear from view. With it went the 'global dialogue of the oppressed' that seemed to offer so much in terms of building a movement. In reality, the WSF was one of the very few opportunities for activists from the global North to encounter activists from the global South and learn about each other's situation and priorities. It was also one of the few examples of a 'global' initiative that the movement had available. Without an event or an initiative of this emblematic kind, activists of necessity retreated back to their own spaces and places. A once 'global' resistance seemed to dissipate into a plurality of resistances that for want of connection to wider struggles once again lapsed into the 'local'.

Network error

With the withering of attendance at the protests at the summits of the global elites and the ebbing fortunes of the WSF, so the support structures that held in place the attention of activists and the media, and which underpinned the sense of there being a movement, began to erode. Networks such as Peoples' Global Action (PGA), Dissent! and ATTAC began to run out of steam as activists weighed up the best use of their time, lost the desire to devote themselves to maintaining the network, or otherwise decided to use their energies for other purposes. Internet sites became neglected, links went dead, the network stalled, reinforcing the impression alluded to above, that local initiatives ceased to have a 'global' significance and reverted to being local in appearance and impact. Peasant rebellions in far-flung corners of the world once again took on the appearance of insurrections at the margin or 'periphery', as opposed to instances of some more generalised rebellion (the 'Fourth World War' as one notable film described it) that somehow dissolved the distinction between core and periphery.

This ebbing of the 'anti-capitalist movement' in the sense of a horizontal network of otherwise autonomous 'hubs' and initiatives reflects both the strength and the weakness of networks. Unlike traditional forms of political organisation such as political parties and lobbying groups, networks have low start-up and maintenance costs. They rely on the availability of a now straight-forward technology combined with the input of what might be a relatively small number of people – certainly in comparison with the staff needed to maintain the office of a political party or NGO. Through maintaining a website, relevant links and some regular updates, an impression can quickly be created of significant activity, reach and influence. Yet, it is precisely these low input costs that also mean that it is easy to pull the plug on these kinds of activities as and when people lose interest in them or when external factors such as the risk of increased surveillance come into play. With virtual nodes and networks it is very much a case of 'easy come, easy go'.

What this means for our purposes is that it is easy to read too much into the network form as a basis for making judgements about the strength and depth of a given political movement, and this includes movements on the right as well as on the left. Neo-Nazis have notoriously caused enormous alarm amongst political commentators for the same reason. A relatively small handful of activists can set up a menacing web presence and air of extensive activity, when the reality on the ground might be that such groups are otherwise insignificant and unable to mobilise more than a few dozen sympathisers. Because it is so easy to give an impression of extensive activity, so it is just as easy to fall into the trap of mistaking the clamour of digital noise for depth of political impact. The equation is more complex than that. It also highlights an important feature of the phenomena we are discussing.

As is becoming increasingly evident, today's radicalism is much more about generating what we might term *resonances* than it is about a linear process of capturing power on the model of traditional radicalisms. Few of today's activists are interested in following the trajectory associated with vertical politics, that is the painstaking development of a programme, mobilising individuals, building political support, standing for election or in some other way organising themselves for power. Today's anti-capitalism is much more complex, ambivalent and multi-layered than this linear model. It embraces all manner of individuals, groups and movements, from those like the Zapatistas engaged in a physical struggle for survival, to those seeking to capture the imaginations and senses of sophisticated consumers unused to the idea of there being some significant flaw in the world as they know it. All these actors are part of the anti-capitalist phenomenon, but their attachment to a movement can be virtual, ephemeral or very real. The prospect of bringing all of this together into one over-arching political project now looks not merely implausible, but based on a mistaken premise: that what the world requires is a single unitary solution to the ills confronting humanity. Even the network or horizontal model is too rigid and fixed to encapsulate this facility of activists to adapt and change the manner and nature of their interactions. What we are describing is less network politics than 'flash' politics, immediate politics, liquid politics – an evanescent series of events, protests, initiatives that ebb and flow, come and go, resonate or not. Something that looks less like the classic Leninist party would be difficult to describe.

A twist in the tale: the GFC and the battle for democracy

By the middle of the first decade of the twenty-first century the anti-capitalist movement seemed to be on the downward slope. Summit protests were beginning to wane in appeal, interest in the WSF had begun to decline, and the virtual network of support and solidarity underpinning the impression of a global movement had stagnated. It was easy to draw the conclusion that for the moment this latest upsurge of militant activity had peaked. But the co-ordinates of this movement ecology were about to change in dramatic ways and from a perhaps unlikely source for the non-committed outsider: capitalism itself. The GFC, which started in 2007 and which led to a severe global recession, provided renewed impetus for capitalism's critics. There is no need here to rehearse the causes and characteristics of that crisis which we have already covered in the first chapter. What we do need to consider, however, is the impact of the GFC in terms of the evolution and trajectory of anti-capitalism. It becomes clear that this latest set of crises has produced a quite different kind of politics even to that documented earlier. Here's how the GFC impacted radical politics.

Occupy everything

The most striking phenomenon to come out of the GFC was the emergence of a politics of occupation inspired by the events of the 'Arab Spring' and in particular the occupation of Tahrir Square in Cairo by those calling for democratic reforms. The latter was not obviously an 'anti-capitalist' protest; but what it highlighted was of relevance *to* anti-capitalists. The complaint was a familiar one in the politics of the developing world. The protestors were calling quite simply for greater democracy than the elite-managed 'representative democracy' that had allowed and encouraged gross inequalities and injustices to multiply through the 'neo-colonial' operation of the free market.

The occupation of Tahrir Square struck a chord across the world. Soon protests were held in Spain, in the UK and on Wall Street, the emblematic epicentre of global financialised capitalism. 'Occupy Wall Street', as the latter phenomenon became known, emerged late in 2011 and provided the chief focal point for this new set of initiatives which rapidly spread across the USA, Europe, the developed world more generally and then back into the developing world. It had a simple message: we, 'the 99%', have been ripped off by the '1%', that is the wealthy plutocrats running the banks, hedge funds, derivatives and other instruments of 'financial mass destruction'.

Over the days and weeks that followed, Occupy became established as an important intervention. Notable was the participants' steadfast refusal to take the first steps down the 'vertical' path of party political organisation. They refused to nominate leaders, a manifesto or an alternative set of demands – or even an alternative analysis. The refusal was wilful and self-conscious. It wasn't that activists were *unable* to come up with alternatives; they chose not to. This was underscored by some of the slogans that emerged. At my local Occupy one slogan read: '#occupysydney is a political statement, not politically affiliated'. In Toronto, one protestor held a placard that read 'slogan pending'. A digital Occupy slogan read 'Calling every protestor a socialist is like calling every woman who won't date you a lesbian' – carefully followed by 'not that there's anything wrong with being a socialist! or being a lesbian'.

There were a number of readings of this set of refusals. From the radical left came the view that these gestures manifested a fear of politics, a fear of moving past the comfortable cocoon of 'activism for activism's sake' towards the much more demanding business of developing a shared analysis and programme that could galvanise support in the wider community. Occupy, so it was claimed, was an introspective and narcissistic initiative that in its refusal to contemplate action, as opposed to occupation, should be seen as complicit in leaving everything as it is. John Lydon, once of the Sex Pistols, predicted that Occupy would end up 'with some hippy playing a flute', which encapsulates some of this critique. Occupy's refusal is the refusal of those who can *afford* to refuse without coming up with a meaningful alternative.

On the other hand, there were those who saw in this very refusal further evidence of the appetite to move away from apparently failed models of radical activity towards a different kind or style of politics – what I described above as *resonant* politics. This is a politics that seeks to pose questions of a profound kind, without limiting the answers that individuals, groups, communities might come up with. It seeks to draw our attention to an injustice, without telling us or dictating to us how we might overcome or address this injustice. It's a politics that seeks to draw our attention to the deficiencies of *politics and the political itself*, by which we mean the normal or mainstream political process including the normal or mainstream forms of opposition. It seeks to induce reflection in ordinary citizens who might otherwise never get around to questioning the terms and conditions of the system of which they are a part. It seeks to create a reaction, to attract attention, to gather force, to encourage us to pose demanding questions. It seeks to create ripples, cracks, fissures in the otherwise smooth functioning of capitalist everyday life.

This is what democracy looks like

The other significant picture of the protests such as Occupy and of those led by the *Indignados* in Spain is the accent on 'true' or 'real' democracy, with the implication that the form of democracy currently on offer is 'false' or 'fictive'. This echoes the analysis offered by heterodox figures such as Noam Chomsky (*Manufacturing Consent*) and before him Herbert Marcuse (*One Dimensional Man*) who argue that liberal democracy fails to live up to the ideals or values we associate with democracy, such as self-rule and autonomy. It also feeds off popular culture and in particular the book and film *V for Vendetta* by Alan Moore that depicts a bleak dystopian future reminiscent of Orwell's *1984*. It fixes on the masked figure of 'V' who somewhat improbably leads a mass insurrection against a decadent regime. The mask in question is that of Guy Fawkes, the Catholic agitator who led the plot to blow up the British Houses of Parliament in 1605. The mask, which had been associated with a group of hacktivists calling themselves the Anonymous collective, was adopted by

Spanish protestors before becoming a worldwide emblem of resistance.

As we have been discussing, the focus for a lot of recent radical activity has been justice, or rather injustice. The anti-capitalist movement rebranded itself as the 'global justice movement' sometime after Seattle, and many of the debates and discussions that took place within forums such as the WSF were about who gets what from present arrangements. There was much discussion of the inequities of 'dumping', 'structural adjustment', 'trickle down economics' and suchlike. After the GFC the focus for activist initiatives around the world changed markedly towards a concern with democracy. Why?

What the GFC revealed was the extent and degree to which the political process had become complicit in the creation of the unsustainable economic and financial model we explored in the first chapter. This is a hyper-financialised form of neoliberalism that combines the outsourcing of previous public goods such as pensions with a radical deregulation of the activities of banks, building societies and financial companies to create what has aptly been termed 'casino capitalism', in which bankers bet our savings and pensions on various improbable and very high risk scenarios. Financialisation was aided and abetted by the political class who had been lobbied by the financial industry to eliminate obstacles and regulations to 'derivatives', in turn the key to unlocking massive financial gains. So the financial crisis was as much a *political* failure as it was a regulatory and legal failure to rein back the risk-taking of banks and the financial services. What protesters were arguing was that neoliberalism had long ago ceased to be one political choice amongst many for the electorate but the dominant ideology of our times. Representative politics had ceased to represent different choices and political alternatives. It had defaulted to the position well documented by early Marxist critics of bourgeois liberal democracy: a system whose primary function is to preserve and protect the interests of the capitalist class. Clearly, in this new phase of protest the object of the demonstrators' anger now moved away from the instruments of global governance such as the WTO and the IMF to encompass political elites at the level of the nation-state.

A further feature of the wave of protests sparked by the GFC was its essentially *defensive* character. The slogan of the anti-capitalist movement emerging from Seattle was, famously, 'Another world is possible!' This demonstrated the idealism, indeed utopianism, of this phase of militant activity across the globe. It was inspired by the dream of a completely different social and economic logic. The protests triggered by the GFC were if anything backward-looking. It was social democracy and the welfare state that had to be protected. This of course reflected the new politics of 'austerity' that accompanied financial catastrophe across much of the globe. In order to prevent a financial meltdown states had had to step in to prop up their own banks using taxpayers' money. The alternative, so it was argued, was a meltdown in the banking system, a loss of people's savings and a financial hiatus resulting in social and economic collapse. Better to run up deficits – albeit of eye-watering proportions – in the near term than see the entire superstructure fall to the ground like a house of cards. However, having run up deficits against the public balance sheet, political elites then found it easy to argue that they needed to make drastic savings against public spending in order to get on top of the crisis. Across the developed world elites were prompted to embark on deficit reduction through cuts in public services, pensions and education. Public investment was often cut too, diminishing demand for new buildings, roads, infrastructure, and in turn suppressing wages and promoting a further spiral of economic decline. Greece, Ireland and Italy, to name but three, were forced to undertake radical cuts to every aspect of social provision, winding back decades of policies designed to improve the welfare and condition of ordinary men and women.

So the effect of austerity was to promote a defensive style of protest and activism that sought in large measure to safeguard the achievements of a previous phase of capitalism, the social democratic or 'welfare' variety associated with the 1960s and 1970s, as opposed to contesting capitalism as such. In this latest phase of radical activism the demand for constructing new or alternative worlds was drowned out in the chorus of demands to protect the already existing world that seems to be threatened by these new developments. The idealistic, utopian currents that had earlier informed militant initiatives was displaced by a more pragmatic and hard-headed concern to promote and protect social democratic values, basic entitlements and existing standards of living. Stéphane Hessel's pamphlet *Indignez-Vous* (literally 'get angry'), which sold several million copies soon after publication in 2010, articulated the point clearly. Ordinary men and women had to defend the welfare state and the humanist values it represented against the onslaught of neoliberalism. Fear of loss was the new fuel for radical activity, protests and demonstrations across Europe and elsewhere – but it was also a fear borne of betrayal. The success of social democracy was based on the idea of a contract between the elites who ran the show and the people, whose hard work and enterprise were required to generate the income for welfare provision. Social democracy enacted a style of elite democracy – but with a purpose: to manage the economy for the needs of everyone. It worked for several decades. But with the GFC an altogether different image emerged: elite autocracy – a style of governance for the rich and by the rich. Democracy, evidently, had been betrayed.

Some conclusions

So what do these recent developments tell us about the state of anti-capitalism? Where is anti-capitalism going?

Firstly, and notwithstanding the astonishing events of the GFC which has caused immense hardship and impoverishment to many across the developed and developing world, there is very little sign of an appetite to develop a traditional oppositional political movement of the kind that we associate with Marxist and socialist parties. We see all sorts of militant gestures and initiatives, such as occupations, flash protests, Twitter-generated mobs and demonstrations. There is a huge amount of activity and creativity in terms of people's responses to the new economic crisis; but what we don't see is a concerted, significant, energetic or imaginative attempt to create a new political party. The 'vertical' model of organisation seems to have become redundant. In the teeth of deep economic crisis, the kind of crisis that Marxists have always seen as a fertile ground for the building of 'the movement', what we have witnessed points in a very different direction, that is toward what Marxists disparagingly call 'spontaneity'. These are activisms without an apparent core organisation or strategy to direct them. They therefore have the appearance of 'flare ups' or 'flash' protests as opposed to set-piece protests featuring a platform of 'leaders' intoning a shared analysis. Of course as the radical theorist Cornelius Castoriadis once put it, 'spontaneity takes a lot of organisation', which as an observation is a useful corrective to the far left's insistence on the necessity for a vanguard to show the masses 'the line of march'. But what it reflects is as much the nature of the technological revolution that we have been referring to throughout the book as it is any particular design or intention on behalf of activists. It is now just much easier to organise protests and demonstrations without the need for a standing bureaucracy or organisation of the classical political party kind. DIY politics has taken off at least partly because it is just so much easier to organise protests and demonstrations than it used to be without all the paraphernalia of party political organisation. Activists don't need offices, printing presses, or elaborate apparatuses of organisation. Nor do they need formally elected or anointed leaders – or they don't *think* they do. Perhaps there will come a moment when this new generation of activists get fed up with their resonant, 'instant', immediate, oppositional politics. But the signs point in the opposite direction: towards *greater* speed, velocity, immediacy, vibrancy, and 'spontaneity'.

Secondly, and as would seem to follow from the above, the linear model of oppositional politics – which insists on building a party, mobilising people behind a manifesto or a program, and seeking power either through the ballot box or through the model of the putsch or seizure of power – seems to be equally redundant. In its place has emerged a style of post-representative politics that seeks to create *resonances*. This is partly a story about technology, but also a story about the media-saturated context of the contemporary political environment. What seems to be the case is that today's activists show little appetite for power. They are motivated less by the prospect of 'taking over' the apparatus of governance than by querying, challenging, mocking those who run it. They don't want to wait, to plan, to strategise. They want to collapse what might be termed the 'temporal lag' of traditional radicalisms – '*Just wait until we get into power* …' – in favour of immediacy. There is too an appetite for the creation of parallel or autonomous initiatives that prefigure alternatives, but whose primary function is to provoke a sense in ordinary people that the world as it exists is not the only world we can imagine. Today's militant activity is much more prefigurative than that of the past. It attracts attention, and in particular it attracts the attention of the media, which can relay an action or event in the blink of an eye around the world. Sometimes these actions amount to nothing or very little; but sometimes they resonate and create the desire for similar kinds of action that stimulate more kinds of activity. It's true that this is a much less predictable model of politics in the sense that it is much less easy to predict what *kind* of action will resonate and what the consequences of that resonance will be. It's a style of politics that makes it more difficult for us to be confident about its effectiveness or impact. The lines of causality are blurred – if not chaotic – compared with the smooth trajectories of linear politics. Nonetheless if we are looking for the common denominator between recent initiatives such as Occupy, the *Indignados*, culture jamming, flash protests and the like, then it is the immediacy of mobilisations – and also their ephemerality or evanescent quality. Events, actions, protests come and go, ebb and flow. Some resonate, some catch the imagination; others don't; some exemplify different possibilities and the availability of different ways of living – others just seem bizarre or irrelevant.

Related to the above is, thirdly, a disavowal of representation and representative politics in all its guises, whether as the style or mode of oppositional politics, or as the governing paradigm in the form of liberal-democratic politics. The unifying demand of the moment is 'true' or 'real' democracy, as opposed to mediated elite representative democracy. This is therefore democracy as 'autonomy', as something *lived and everyday*, as opposed to democracy as a spectacle beamed into our living rooms, something we read about, something we engage in once every four or five years when elites are 'rotated' to deploy the dull language of political science. Representative democracy might be, as Churchill famously noted, 'the least worst' form of rule that we have come up with so far, but it is one seen as deeply implicated in the financial catastrophe of the GFC, a democracy that serves the needs of the market, banks, plutocrats, 'the 1%'. It is a form of democracy that is rapidly losing credibility in the eyes of ordinary people, who vote less, join political parties in dramatically reduced numbers, trust their politicians less, and show diminishing interest in the affairs and doings of the political elites. If there is a theme to today's anti-capitalism, then it is the demand for *self-governance* – for a democracy of, for and by the people, not their proxies.

Old hands will of course see this less as a break with the past than as reconnective to the concerns of earlier generations of anarchists, socialists and indeed Marxists, nearly all of whom put great emphasis on the recuperation of social power from elites and the development of democracy or autonomy as a *lived activity*, as opposed to a spectacle or ritual of the kind many critics say democracy has become. Both Marx and Lenin, for example, were insistent that democracy was a system of 'associated production', by which they meant that all aspects of social functioning became the subject matter and common concern of all citizens. It was Marx who wrote glowingly of the anarchic experiment of the Paris Commune of 1871 that enacted a kind of hyper-democracy combining regular rotation of office with the rough and ready participation of ordinary citizens in all manner of decision-making. It was Lenin who wrote in similar terms in *State and Revolution* about the first Soviet councils that sprang up in the heady days of early 1917. 'All Power to the Soviets' has a wonderfully antique ring to it; but it evokes in substantive terms a similar sentiment as the demand for 'true' or 'real' democracy does today: the idea of a democracy that is *real*, that engages all of us, the ordinary men and women – the 99% – in the key decisions facing our communities. Of course we could query the commitment over the decades of many Marxists to these democratic and libertarian ideals; but the point is that classical anti-capitalists like Marx and Lenin were deeply critical of 'bourgeois' democracy for more or less identical reasons to those we find articulated by today's disaffiliated activists. Could it be, paradoxically, that the latter are on the verge of rediscovering and reconnecting with perhaps the most persistent demand of the classical anti-capitalist tradition, one that in so many other respects it has sought to distance itself from? That demand is, quite simply, for democracy – *real or true democracy*. As ever, only time will tell.

Contemporary anti-capitalism: a timeline

The following represents a highly selective list of recent events to give readers some idea of how major events and initiatives mentioned in the book relate to each other chronologically.

1998

May   Meeting of WTO in Geneva and 'M16' (for May 16) Day of Action

October   Paris Citizens Summit Against the Multilateral Agreement on Investment (MAI).

1999

June   'Cologne99' EU and G8 summit.
J18 (June 18) Global Day of Action – extensive demonstrations and marches around the world.

December   WTO Ministerial meeting in **Seattle** – N30 Global Action Day – 'The Turtles and Teamsters' march – street battles – (media) birth of the anti-capitalist/anti-globalisation movement.

2000

April   Meeting of the IMF and World Bank in **Washington DC** to discuss structural adjustment policies and austerity measures for Mexico and Haiti – large demonstrations.

June   Meeting of the Organisation of American States in Windsor, Ontario – demonstrations and large numbers arrested.

Demonstrations in Millau, France against the arrest of José Bové and others for wrecking a McDonald's restaurant – debates and workshops.

September   WEF meets in **Melbourne**, Australia – S11 Day of Action – massive demonstrations.

Meeting of the IMF in **Prague** – S26 Global Day of Action – extensive street battles.

December   EU summit in **Nice** – massive demonstrations.

2001

January   Meeting of the WEF in Davos, Switzerland shadowed by meeting of the first WSF in Porto Alegre, Brazil, hosted by Brazilian Workers' Party and French journal *Le Monde diplomatique*.

March   Zapatistas march to Mexico City demanding rights for indigenous groups and resolution of the land question.

April   WTO Meeting in **Quebec City**, Canada – A20 Global Day of Action against 'Summit of the Americas' – extensive arrests and violence against protestors.

June   World Bank Meeting in **Barcelona** – cancelled due to threat of 'disorder'. Street parties and demonstrations take place anyway.

July   G8 meeting in **Genoa** – one of the most violent protests since the new wave of activism – protestor Carlo Guiliani shot dead and run over by police van.

| September | '9/11': World Bank and IMF meetings cancelled. |
| November | WTO meeting in **Qatar** to discuss intellectual property rights (the 'Doha Round'). |

2002

January	Meeting of WEF in New York with extensive demonstrations and protests; second WSF meeting at Porto Alegre, Brazil.
April	Meeting of World Bank and IMF in **Washington DC** – A20 Day of Action – extensive demonstrations.
June	G8 summit in **Kananaskis, Canada** – despite extreme remoteness of location there are still demonstrations.
August	Foro Social Mundial, Argentina – anti-globalisation convergence to discuss strategies to confront austerity measures.
September	World Bank and IMF meetings in **Washington DC** – S26 Day of Action.
October	International Indigenous Day in Latin America – convergence to discuss shared problems of indigenous groups and strategies to confront elites.
	O20 Day of Action in Latin America – extensive demonstrations in **Quito** and elsewhere.
	Global Day of Action Against War – 'Not in Our Name' marches across the world.
	Encuentro Continental in Equador: 'Another America is Possible'.
November	First European Social Forum, Italy.
	WTO meeting in Sydney, Australia – demonstrations.
	'Buy Nothing Day'.
December	Global Day of Action for Argentina – demonstrations and marches across the world.

2003

January	First Asian Social Forum, Hyderabad, India.
	Third WSF, Porto Alegre, Brazil.
April	Mobilisation against US intervention in Latin America and the Caribbean, Washington DC.
	Meetings of the World Bank and IMF, Washington DC – demonstrations.
	First Oceania Social Forum, New Zealand.
June	G8 summit, **Evian**, France – Day of Action – extensive demonstrations.
	EU summit, Greece – extensive demonstrations.
July	South Asian Peasants' Assembly – massive convergence to discuss regional strategy of resistance.
August	'Larzac 2003': extensive anti-capitalist festival organised by *Confédération Paysanne* near Millau.
September	Global Week of Action against the WTO.
	Fifth WTO Ministerial, **Cancun**, Mexico. Major demonstrations across the world. Suicide of Korean farmer, Lee Kyung-hae.
October	Second Oceania Social Forum, Wellington, New Zealand.
November	Second European Social Forum, Paris, France.

2004

January	Fourth WSF, Mumbai, India.
April	Global Day of Action.
July	Americas Social Forum, Quito, Ecuador.
October	European Social Forum, London.

2005

January	Fifth WSF, Porto Alegre, Brazil.

March	Global Action Day for Peace.
July	G8 summit, **Gleneagles**, Scotland – extensive protests and events around the idea of 'Make Poverty History', including rock concerts and events across five continents.
October	Week of Action against G8.
December	WTO Ministerial in Hong Kong – extensive protests.

2006

January	Zapatistas launch the 'Otra Campana' to seek alliances against neoliberalism amongst civil society groups in the run-up to the Mexican presidential elections.
	Sixth WSF – polycentric with meetings in Caracas (Venezuala), Bamako (Mali) and Karachi (India).
February	European protests against the Bolkestein Directive launched by the EU.
March	Global Action Days against war in Iraq.
June	First USA Social Forum.
July	G8 summit protests in **St Petersburg**, Russia.
December	International Encuentro hosted by the Zapatistas for the peoples of the world.

2007

January	WSF held in Nairobi, Kenya.
	Massive anti-war protests in the USA.
June	G8 summit, Heiligendamm, Germany.

2008

January	WSF 'Global Day of Action'.
July	Riots break out across the Middle East and developing world over the cost of food and basic necessities. Political demands for greater democracy follow.

September   Collapse of Lehman Brothers – often seen as the moment when the incipient global financial crisis hit the consciousness of citizens around the world.

2009

January   WSF holds an event at Belem in Brazil focusing on the plight of indigenous, landless and stateless peoples.

2010

January   Decentralised WSF with various events occurring globally, including well-attended US Social Forum in Detroit.

April   G20 **London** protests – bystander Ian Tomlinson killed by police officer.

June   G20 **Toronto** protests.

December   Uprisings across the Middle East, later termed the 'Arab Spring', against autocratic regimes across the region.

2011

January   WSF held in Dakar, Senegal.

May   15-M movement (also called the *Indignados*) calls for occupations and mobilisation in Spanish cities against austerity cuts and in favour of 'Real Democracy'.

September   Occupy Wall St initiated – Occupy actions quickly multiply across the US and beyond.

October   Global Day of Action against cuts and austerity.

2012

January   WSF held in Porto Alegre, Brazil.

Glossary of key terms, thinkers and movements

anarchism   Umbrella term for all those who reject the state and 'statism', the belief that state-like structures are inevitable or necessary to maintain order. Anarchists have also tended to reject the Marxian idea of the revolutionary party and 'dictatorship of the proletariat' as the basis for creating a new order. Anarchists are suspicious of most claims to authority and regard ordinary people's capacity for self-organisation as a natural or desirable basis for any social order. Anarchism is otherwise a highly diverse tradition.

autonomism   A hybrid of Marxism, anarchism and several other currents of thought such as Situationism and environmentalism. Associated with the outright rejection of the state in favour of councils, soviets or other directly participatory forms of organisation. Accords primacy to class struggle and the capacity of all people to organise themselves for the purpose of resistance and communal organisation. The best known autonomist thinkers are Antonio Negri and John Holloway.

Subcomandante Insurgente Marcos   Leading thinker, poet and philosopher of the Zapatistas, who also goes by the name Delegate Zero. Associated with 'Zapatismo', which rejects conventional revolutionary doctrine, the idea of the vanguard party and the leading role of intellectuals in anti-capitalist struggles. Many of his speeches and writings are collected in *The Word Is Our Weapon*.

Marxism The doctrine or philosophy held by Marxists. Marxism is an umbrella term for the numerous competing currents and tendencies such as Leninism, Trotskyism and Maoism that have sought to further refine Marx's work for practical purposes. Marxism emphasises the centrality of class struggle to revolutionary change and the necessity for the abolition of the market and the private ownership of the means of production. It also posits an ideal end point, 'communism', as distinct from 'socialism' which is regarded as a 'transition' period leading to communism.

neoliberalism In terms of ideas, neoliberalism represents the reassertion of the classical liberal concern to promote the maximum possible liberty and/or the maximum possible economic efficiency. In terms of politics, neoliberalism is associated with the rise to power of Mrs Thatcher in the UK and Ronald Reagan in the USA. However, in the 1970s and 1980s neoliberalism quickly established itself as the ideology of choice for global elites generally, and the institutions of global governance such as the IMF more particularly. Neoliberalism in the contemporary context is asserted through the requirement to open markets and services to competition, to rein back public spending, and to endorse the commodification of the global 'commons', i.e. through gene patenting and the protection of intellectual property rights.

Occupy Occupy is the umbrella term for the various interconnected real and virtual occupations created in the wake of the global financial crisis (GFC) and Arab Spring in 2011. The most written-about of these is Occupy Wall Street which took over Zuccotti Park in New York in late 2011. However, the movement spawned hundreds of occupations across the world, some of which have semi-permanent features. Occupy is notable for resisting the development of a programme or ideology, leadership and a developed bureaucracy or set of offices. The suggestion here is that this is a new species of 'resonant' politics – a politics designed to provoke debate and discussion, rather than supply solutions.

Situationism A hybrid of autonomist Marxism, surrealism and existentialism associated with French radicals, Guy Debord and Raoul Vaneigem. Like autonomism, situationism rejects revolutionary parties and vanguards, holding that revolutionary moments are not manufactured, but distinct 'situations' in which otherwise suppressed desires, frustrations and creativity can break loose, creating the conditions in which self-organisation can become a reality. Situationists stress the necessity for a popular counter-aesthetic to capitalism, ideas which can be found today in the outlook and activities of 'adbusting' and 'subvertising'.

social democracy This term was initially associated with the German and Austrian socialists of the late nineteenth century who followed an electoral and parliamentary strategy – as opposed to the revolutionary strategy urged by figures such as Lenin. Social democracy is now associated with the idea of making market economies work to the benefit of the many rather than the few. This is achieved through state intervention to promote economic growth and redistribution to ensure social equality and welfare provision.

World Bank This was set up alongside the IMF as part of the Bretton Woods settlement at the end of the Second World War. It finances development and reconstruction projects, and is a focus for protests because of the harsh terms set for repayment of loans which often leave already impoverished nations even poorer.

World Economic Forum (WEF) Normally meeting in Davos, Switzerland on an annual basis, the WEF is a private association paid for by the subscriptions of large corporations. It promotes 'dialogue', largely among the wealthy, though speakers from the developing world are usually invited as well. It acts as an informal lobbying group urging national governments and global institutions to promote the private sector and corporate interests generally.

World Social Forum (WSF) This initiative was launched in 2000 (first meeting in January 2001) by members of ATTAC and the Brazilian Workers' Party to provide an alternative viewpoint on global affairs to the WEF. It quickly mushroomed into a vast carnival meeting every January, and has also spawned regional and national social forums around the world, which similarly meet on an annual basis.

World Trade Organisation (WTO) Set up in 1995 to give an institutional focus for the General Agreement on Tariffs and Trade negotiations which have been on-going since the Second World War. The object of the negotiations is the development of a 'level playing field' for global trade, the idea being that increased trade will lead to increased wealth across the globe (otherwise known as 'trickle-down theory'). It is a major focus for anti-capitalist demonstrations because of the manner in which the North has successively protected its own interests at the cost of the developing world through 'trickle-up' measures such as the dumping of subsidised goods, gene patenting and preferential trading arrangements between wealthy nations.

Zapatistas (EZLN) The army of national liberation that took over the Chiapas region in the wake of the 1994 signing of the North America Free Trade Area (NAFTA) agreement. Since 1994 the Zapatistas have established a zone of forty or so communities which run on a directly democratic basis. They have also sought to broaden their struggle and are frequent participants in pan-American and global 'convergences'.

Resources

Introduction

Emma Bircham and John Charlton (eds), *Anti-Capitalism: A Guide to the Movement* (London: Bookmarks, 2001)

Alex Callinicos, *An Anti-Capitalist Manifesto* (Cambridge: Polity Press, 2003)

Paul Kingsnorth, *One No, Many Yes: A Journey to the Heart of the Global Resistance Movement* (London: Free Press, 2003)

Naomi Klein, *No Logo* (London: Flamingo, 2000)

Naomi Klein, *Fences and Windows* (London: Flamingo, 2002)

Paul Mason, *Meltdown: The End of the Age of Greed* (London: Verso, 2010)

Paul Mason, *Why It's Kicking Off Everywhere: The New Global Revolutions* (London: Verso, 2012)

George Monbiot, *The Age of Consent* (London: Flamingo, 2003)

Gregory Palast, *The Best Democracy Money Can Buy* (London: Robinson, 2002)

Amory Starr, *Naming the Corporate Enemy: Anti-Corporate Movements Confront Globalization* (London, Zed Books, 2000)

Link to:

www.naomiklein.org
www.monbiot.com
www.michaelmoore.com
www.gregpalast.com

Watch:

Inside Job (2010) – the story of the global financial crisis

The Take (2004) – Naomi Klein's account of the collapse of the Argentinian economy and how it inspired a movement to take over defunct factories

Capitalism: A Love Story (2009) – Michael Moore's exposé of the financial crisis

Žižek! (2005) – documentary profiling the world's most prominent anti-capitalist philosopher

Bush Family Fortunes: The Best Democracy Money Can Buy (2004) – Greg Palast's exposé of the Bush oligarchs

Chapter 1

Noam Chomsky, *Profit over People: Neoliberalism and Global Order* (New York: Seven Stories Press, 1998)

Milton Friedman, *Capitalism and Freedom* (Chicago: University of Chicago Press, 2002 [1962])

Thomas Friedman, *The World Is Flat: A Brief History of the Twenty-First Century* (New York: Picador, 2007)

David Harvey, *A Brief History of Neoliberalism* (Oxford: Oxford University Press, 2007)

David Held and Anthony McGrew, *Globalization/Anti-Globalization* (Oxford and Malden, MA: Polity, 2002)

Eric Hobsbawm, *Age of Extremes: The Short Twentieth Century* (London: Abacus, 1994)

Karl Marx and Friedrich Engels, *The Communist Manifesto* [1848] www.marxists.org/archive/marx/works/1848/communist-manifesto

Paul Mason, *Meltdown: The End of the Age of Greed* (London: Verso, 2010)

Allan Melzer, *Why Capitalism?* (Oxford: Oxford University Press, 2012)

Judith Sklair, *Globalization: Capitalism and its Alternatives* (Oxford and New York: Oxford University Press, 2002)

Adam Smith, *The Wealth of Nations*, 2 vols. [1776], various editions. Full text available online at: www.econlib.org/library/Smith/smWN.html

Joseph Stiglitz, *Globalization and Its Discontents* (London: Penguin, 2002)

Link to:

www.capitalism.org
www.en.wikipedia.org/wiki/Portal:Capitalism
www.libcom.org
www.wto.org
www.worldbank.org
www.oecd.org
www.unctad.org

Watch:

The Corporation (2003) – documentary examining the origins and role of corporations

Wall Street (1987) – semi-fictional account concerning the ethics of Wall Steet bankers

Trading Places (1983) – comedy in which a down-and-out trades places with a banker

Avatar (2009) – James Cameron's blockbuster parable concerning conquest and colonialism

Chapter 2

Manuel Castells, *The Rise of the Network Society* (London: Wiley, 2009)

Harry Cleaver, 'Computer-linked social movements and the global threat to capitalism', www.eco.utexas.edu/homepages/faculty/Cleaver/polnet.html

Alexander Cockburn and Jeffrey St Clair, *Five Days that Shook the World: The Battle for Seattle and Beyond* (London and New York: Verso, 2000)

Guy Debord, *The Society of the Spectacle* (London: Rebel Press, 1971 [1967]). Full text available online at: www.nothingness.org

Jo Freeman, *We Will Be Heard: Women's Struggles for Political Power in the United States* (New York: Rowman & Littlefield, 2008)

Francis Fukuyama, *The End of History and the Last Man* (London and New York: Penguin, 1992)

Eric Hobsbawm, *The New Century* (London: Abacus, 2000)

Mark Kurlansky, *1968: The Year that Rocked the World* (New York: Random House, 2005)

Jean-François Lyotard, *The Postmodern Condition* (Minneapolis: University of Minnesota Press, 1984)

Angelo Quattrochi and Tom Nairn, *The Beginning of the End: France, May 1968* ((London and New York: Verso, 1998)

Donald Sassoon, *One Hundred Years of Socialism* (London: Fontana, 1996)

Tiziana Terranova, *Network Culture, Politics for the Information Age* (London: Pluto, 2004)

Raoul Vaneigem, *The Revolution of Everyday Life* (London: Rebel Press, 1994 [1967]). Full text available online at: www.nothingness.org

McKenzie Wark, *The Beach Beneath the Street: The Everyday Life and Glorious Times of the Situationist International* (London: Verso, 2011)

Link to:

www.nothingness.org (situationist texts)
www.newleftreview.org
www.adbusters.org
www.greenpeace.org
www.foe.org (Friends of the Earth, USA)
www.foe.co.uk
www.indymedia.org

www.cultdeadcow.com (hacktivist site and portal)
www.hacktivismo.com
www.globalexchange.org
www.occupywallst.org
www.jofreeman.com (articles on women's lib, radical social movements)
www.mstbrazil.org (Sem Terra)

Watch:

Society of the Spectacle (1973) – Guy Debord's experimental film based
on the book of the same name
V for Vendetta (2005) – based on Alan Moore's dystopian novel, the film
used the now iconic Guy Fawkes mask as a trope for resistance to
totalitarianism
The Yes Men Fix the World (2009) – the exploits of high profile culture
jammers
This Is What Democracy Looks Like (2000) – documentary examining the
events around the Seattle protests in 1999
The Fourth World War (2003) – documentary examining neoliberal governance around the world and the nature of the resistances to it

Chapter 3

Zygmunt Bauman, *The Individualized Society* (Oxford: Polity Press,
2001)
Walden Bello, *De-Globalization: Ideas for a New World Economy* (London:
Zed Books, 2003)
Richard Falk, *Predatory Globalization: A Critique* (Oxford: Polity Press,
1999)
Liza Featherstone, *Students Against Sweatshops: The Making of a Movement*
(London and New York: Verso, 2000)
David Held et al., *Global Transformations: Politics, Economics and Culture*
(Cambridge: Polity Press, 1999)

Will Hutton, *The World We're In* (London: Little Brown, 2002)

Immanuel Kant, *Perpetual Peace* [1795], various editions. Full text available online at: www.constitution.org/kant/perpeace.htm

George Monbiot, *The Age of Consent* (London: Flamingo, 2003)

Martha Nussbaum, *Creating Capabilities: The Human Development Approach* (New Haven, CN: Harvard UP, 2011)

Thomas Pogge, *World Poverty and Human Rights* (Oxford: Polity, 2008)

Robert Puttnam, *Bowling Alone: The Collapse and Revival of American Community* (New York: Simon & Schuster, 2001)

Amartya Sen, *The Idea of Justice* (New Haven, CN: Harvard University Press, 2011)

Link to:

www.monbiot.org

www.nosweat.org.uk

www.jubileedebtcampaign.org.uk

www.wdm.org.uk (World Development Movement)

www.oxfam.org

www.focusweb.org (Focus on the Global South)

www.icftu.org (International Confederation of Free Trade Unions)

www.ilo.org (International Labour Organization)

www.confederationpaysanne.fr

www.mondediplo.com (English language edition of *Le Monde diplomatique*)

www.attac.org

www.forumsocialmundial.org.br (World Social Forum)

Watch:

Favela Rising (2005) – documentary about the emergence of a community action programme in the slums of Rio

The End of Poverty (2008) – documentary featuring public intellectuals such as Amartya Sen and Joseph Stiglitz debating why poverty is endemic to global development

New Rulers of the World (2001) – John Pilger's exposé of global capitalism

The Commanding Heights (2002) – PBS-sponsored documentary examining the evolution of capitalism over the course of the twentieth century

Chapter 4

Michael Albert, *ParEcon: Life After Capitalism* (London and New York: Verso, 2003)

Mikhail Bakunin, 'Marxism, Freedom and the State' (1867), various editions available online

Alex Callinicos, *The Revolutionary Ideas of Karl Marx* (London: Bookmarks, 1995)

Andrew Dobson, *Green Political Thought* (London: Routledge, 1995)

Michael Hardt and Antonio Negri, *Empire* (Cambridge, MA: Harvard University Press, 2000)

Michael Hardt and Antonio Negri, *Multitude* (London: Penguin, 2005)

Michael Hardt and Antonio Negri, *Commonwealth* (Cambridge, MA: Harvard University Press, 2011)

John Holloway and Eloine Pelaez (eds), *Zapatista: Reinventing Revolution in Mexico* (London: Pluto Press, 1998)

John Holloway, *Change the World Without Taking Power* (London: Pluto, 2005)

Ruth Kinna, *Anarchism: A Beginner's Guide* (Oxford: Oneworld, 2005)

Subcomandante Insurgente Marcos, *Our Word is Our Weapon: Selected Writings* (London: Serpent's Tail, 2002)

Peter Marshall, *Demanding the Impossible: A History of Anarchism* ((London: Fontana Press, 1993)

William Morris, *News from Nowhere* (1890), various editions

E.F. Schumacher, *Small is Beautiful: Economics as if People Mattered* (London: Vintage, 1993 [1973])

Peter Singer, *Marx: A Very Short Introduction* (Oxford: Oxford University Press, 2001)

John Zerzan, *Future Primitive and Other Essays* (New York: Semiotext(e), 1994)

Slavoj Žižek, *Living in the End Times* (London: Verso, 2011)

Link to:

www.marxists.org

www.marxism.org

www.swp.org.uk (Socialist Workers Party, UK)

www.struggle.ws (libertarian and Zapatista resources)

www.dwardmac.pitzer.edu/Anarchist_Archives (classic anarchist texts)

www.zcommunications.org (left-liberal and ParEcon resources)

www.earthfirst.org

www.greenanarchy.org

www.schnews.org.uk (collation of direct action news and events in the UK)

Watch:

Reds (1981) – notable dramatisation of communist journalist John Reed's involvement with the Bolshevik Revolution

Land and Freedom (1995) – film directed by Ken Loach exploring the events of the Spanish Civil War though the eyes of young communist David Carr

Rosa Luxemburg (1986) – critically acclaimed account of the life of one of the key Marxist figures of the early twentieth century

A Place Called Chiapas (1998) – Canadian documentary investigating the origins and outcomes of the Zapatista rebellion

Zapatista (1999) – an excellent introduction to the Zapatistas, where they have come from and what they represent

Chapter 5

Anon ('The Invisible Committee'), *The Coming Insurrection* (New York: Semiotext, 2009)

Alain Badiou, *The Rebirth of History:Times of Riots and Uprisings* (London: Verso, 2012)

Alex Callinicos, 'Regroupment, Realignment and the Revolutionary Left' – various online locations

Cornelius Castoriadis, 'The Working Class and Organization' [1959] www.marxists.org/archive/castoriadis/1959/organisation.htm

Noam Chomsky, *Manufacturing Consent* (New York: Pantheon, 2011)

Stephane Hessel, *Indignez-Vous!* (Montpellier: Indigene, 2010) – translated as *Time for Outrage*

Naomi Klein, 'What's Next?' in *Fences and Windows* (London: Flamingo, 2002)

Vladimir Ilyich Lenin, *The State and Revolution* [1917] various editions; online at: http://www.marxists.org/archive/lenin/works/1917/staterev/index.htm

John Lydon, '76 minutes with … John Lydon', *Guardian* (31 May 2012), www.guardian.co.uk/culture/2012/may/31/john-lydon-sex-pistols-pil-interview

Herbert Marcuse, *One Dimensional Man* (New York: Beacon Press, 1991)

Karl Marx, *The Civil War in France* [1871] various editions; online at: http://www.marxists.org/archive/marx/works/1871/civil-war-france/ch05.htm

Alan Moore, *V for Vendetta* (New York:Vertigo, 2008)

Jai Sen (ed.), *The World Social Forum: Challenging Empires* (Delhi:Viveka, 2004)

Jai Sen (ed.), *A Political Programme for the World Social Forum? Democracy, Substance and Debate in the Bamako Appeal and the Global Justice Movements* (Delhi: Cacim, 2007)

Slavoj Žižek, *The Year of Dreaming Dangerously* (London:Verso, 2012)

Link to:

www.infoshop.org (contains a useful digest of alternative views on (dis) organisation and horizontal activisms)

www.occupywallst.org

www.occupytogether.org

www.theindignados.org

www.roarmag.org

www.choike.org (independent data collection and analysis relating to the WSF)

www.falseeconomy.org.uk (collection of anti-austerity resources)

Watch:

Rise Like Lions: OWS and the Seeds of Revolution (2011) – documentary film exploring the events around the creation of the Occupy movement in the US

Occupy Unmasked (2012) – provocative spoiler offering a contrarian view of Occupy

Capitalism Is Not in Crisis; Capitalism Is the Crisis (2012) – documentary examining capitalism after the GFC and the resistances around the world contesting post-GFC austerity and budget cuts

Index